Thank you for sharing
yourselves and your
beautiful piece of earth
with us.

Love,

John and Janice
January 1994

EARTH PRAYERS

Books of related interest from HarperSanFrancisco

Peace Prayers
Edited by
The Staff of Harper San Francisco

*Mother Earth Spirituality: Native American Paths
to Healing Ourselves and Our World*
by Ed McGaa, Eagle Man

*A Passion for This Earth: Exploring a New Partnership
of Man, Woman & Nature*
by Valerie Andrews

*To Honor the Earth: Reflections on Living
in Harmony with Nature*
by Dorothy Maclean and Kathleen Thormod Carr

EARTH
PRAYERS

FROM AROUND THE WORLD

365 PRAYERS, POEMS, AND INVOCATIONS FOR HONORING THE EARTH

Edited by
Elizabeth Roberts and Elias Amidon

HarperSanFrancisco
A Division of HarperCollins*Publishers*

Harper San Francisco and the authors, in association with the Rainforest Action Network, will facilitate the planting of two trees for every one tree used in the manufacture of this book.

EARTH PRAYERS. *From Around the World, 365 Prayers, Poems, and Invocations for Honoring the Earth.* Copyright © 1991 by Elizabeth Roberts and Elias Amidon. All rights reserved. Printed in the United States of America. No part of this book may be used or reproduced in any manner whatsoever without written permission except in the case of brief quotations embodied in critical articles and reviews. For information, address HarperCollins Publishers, 10 East 53rd Street, New York, NY 10022.

Acknowledgments begin on p. 440.

COVER DESIGN BY TOM MORGAN AT BLUE DESIGN
COVER PHOTOGRAPH COURTESY OF PANORAMIC STOCK IMAGES
BOOK DESIGN AND ILLUSTRATION BY IRENE IMFELD
COMPOSITION AND PRODUCTION BY WILSTED & TAYLOR

ISBN 0–06–250888–1 (cloth)

An Earlier Edition of this Book Was Cataloged as Follows:

Earth prayers : from around the world, 365 prayers, poems, and
  invocations for honoring the earth / edited by Elizabeth Roberts &
  Elias Amidon. — 1st ed.
      p.   cm.
    ISBN 0–06–250746–X (pbk.)
    1. Earth—Religious aspects.   2. Earth—Prayer-books and
  devotions—English.   3. Nature—Religious aspects.   4. Nature—
  Prayer-books and devotions—English.   5. Devotional calendars.
  I. Roberts, Elizabeth.   II. Amidon, Elias.
  BL438.2.E29   1991
  291.2'12—dc20   90—55790
                                                                CIP

93 94 95 96 HAD 15 14 13 12 11

This edition is printed on acid-free paper that meets the American National Standards Institute Z39.48 Standard.

This book is dedicated to
our children:

Jesse, Hanah, Aura, and Aquila

❧

May the Earth always
speak to your
spirit.

CONTENTS

Part IV • HEALING THE WHOLE • 89

Part V • THE ELEMENTS • 127

CONTENTS

Part VI • BLESSINGS AND INVOCATIONS • 169

Introduction • Mary Rogers • Atharva Veda XIX • Nancy Wood Rig Veda I • Ute prayer • East African Medical Missionary Sisters Zuni prayer • Hawaiian prayer • Jo Poore • Chinook Psalter Doreen Valiente • Walt Franklin • Lois Wickenhauser Sioux prayer • Jane Pellowski • May Sarton Maria Eugenia Baz Ferreira • Traditional Native American prayer Sioux prayer • Saint Patrick • Diann Neu • José Arguëlles Annie Besant • Pawnee/Osage/Omaha song • Diane di Prima Chinook Psalter • Pierre Teilhard de Chardin • Ashanti prayer Traditional Irish blessing • Diann Neu • Donald Jeffrey Hayes Leopold Sedar Senghor • Edward Abbey • Helen Weaver

Part VII • PRAISE AND THANKSGIVING • 211

Introduction • Homeris Hymns XXX • Walt Whitman Ernesto Cardenal • Gerard Manley Hopkins • African canticle Rainer Maria Rilke • Denise Levertov • Ishpriya R.S.C.J. Ernesto Cardenal • Carl Sandburg • Saint Francis of Assisi North American Conference on Christianity and Ecology Gregory Petrov • Harriet Kofalk • Gary Snyder • Iroquois prayer Dolores La Chapelle • Pawnee Hako ceremony • e. e. cummings Thich Nhat Hanh • Paul Winter • W. S. Merwin

Part VIII • BENEDICTION FOR
THE ANIMALS • 247

Part X • THE DAILY ROUND • 331

Introduction
GREETING THE DAY
Cedric Wright • Rumi • Yang Lian
Mescalero Apache song • Thich Nhat Hanh • Hopi song
Thule Eskimo song • Iglulik Eskimo song • Mary Austin
Tecumseh • Eleanor Farjean • Daniel Berrigan
Congregation of Abraxas • Congregation of Abraxas
Pawnee prayer • Ishpriya R.S.C.J.
Sanskrit Salutation to the dawn
Denise Levertov • D. H. Lawrence
GRACES
Ojai School • Unitarian prayer • Edward Espe Brown
Mahanirvana Tantra X • Zen prayer • Thich Nhat Hanh
Arapaho grace • Congregation of Abraxas • John Lame Deer
Gary Snyder • Rabbi Rami M. Shapiro • Marcia Falk
Judith Morley • Alla Renee Bozarth • Starhawk • Luisah Teish
GATHAS
Hildegard of Bingen • Thich Nhat Hanh • Nakagawa Soen-roshi
W. E. B. Du Bois • Kiddushin 4:12 • Hindu prayer
Dedication to Richard St. Barbe Baker • Hasidic saying
Robert Aitken • Anonymous • Guru Angad • Unitarian prayer
Anonymous • Chinook Psalter • Chinook Psalter
Alamsaeen • Lew Welch • Rabbi Abraham Heschel
Navajo chant • Hazrat Inayat Khan • Wendell Berry
Thich Nhat Hanh • Saint Thomas More

THANKS

THIS BOOK BELONGS TO
the hundreds of people who helped us hold its vision over the past
five years.

In particular, we want to thank four people who have nurtured in us
the Earthy spirituality behind this work: Thomas Berry, Passionist
priest and geologian; Joanna Macy, eco-feminist and Earth activist;
Thich Nhat Hanh, Vietnamese poet and Buddhist monk; and Mur-
shid Fazal Inayat-Khan, Sufi master and psychotherapist.

Many other individuals and communities have been of special help
in preparing the manuscript. They aided us in our search for material, shared their experiences with Earth liturgy, and helped create
the interfaith quality of this work. We wish to thank especially
Mary Rogers and the people from One Bamboo Hermitage; the
Jyotiniketan Community; Helvecio Mendes and the University of
Manila; Nancy Wadel, Lee Henderson, and the Chinook Learning Center; Danny Martin and the United Nations Environmental
Sabbath Program; the North American Conference on Christianity
and Ecology; Ralph Metzner and the Green Earth Foundation; Ar-
nie Kotler and the people from Plum Village, France; Wendy John-
son and the Green Gulch Zen Center; Sawan Ashram, Delhi; Rabbi
Rami M. Shapiro and Temple Beth Or; the Congregation of
Abraxas; Dean James Morton and the Cathedral of St. John the

Divine; Ellen Bernstein and Shomrei Adamah; David Brower, Bill Travers, and Earth Island Institute; Dianne Neu and the Women's Alliance for Theology, Ethics, and Ritual; Alla Renee Bozarth; the Smithsonian Institute's Bureau of American Ethnology; the Ojai Foundation School; and the Naropa Institute.

We also wish to acknowledge the contributions of the many unknown native people whose words and wisdom grace each chapter of this book. Their clear voices are a constant reminder that Earth Prayer is a part of daily life. They have much to teach us all.

The personal commitment and kindness of Mark Salzwedel, Caroline Pincus, and Michael Toms of HarperSanFrancisco was especially appreciated through the difficult stages of this book's creation.

The last kudos go to poet Joe Richey and peace activist Kelly Pugh. It was their long days at the library and months over the computer—plus the inspiration of their friendship and their commitment to excellence—that made this book the one you now hold in your hands.

Our deepest gratitude to you all.

THANKSGIVING DAY, 1990
ELIZABETH AND ELIAS, THE EDITORS

A CALL TO
EARTH PRAYER

WE NEED TO PRAY," ELIAS said one afternoon. We both sat silent. Pray? What did that mean to us? We had long since wandered from the traditions of our early religious teachings. While we meditated regularly and valued times of silence and contemplation, the notion of *prayer* awakened in us a new desire—the desire for a communal liturgy directed toward healing human-Earth relations. We wanted to link our personal spiritual life with that of the entire biosphere. Perhaps everything prays—not only humans.

This book is a call to prayer. Several years ago, as we began to grasp the extent of the damage being done to the Earth's life systems, we were filled with deep sadness. So much is being lost—so much richness and natural beauty that our children will never know, perhaps never even miss! How can we heal all that we have disrupted and polluted? Of course, our society and our daily lives have to change. Yet the healing of our relationship with this planet ultimately needs to emerge from our hearts and our spirits.

The idea empowered us. We found ourselves looking through bookstores for prayer traditions that might capture what was in our hearts. Several journals and magazines offered to print our call for "Prayers for the Earth." People responded from the Philippines and from Nicaragua, from Iowa and from New York City. People we had never met searched through the Rig Vedas for us. Others made us aware of the profound reform going on in Hebrew and Christian liturgical traditions. They sent us their favorite poems and blessings. They thanked us. Unknowingly, they healed our despair.

> *The beauty of the trees,*
> *the softness of the air,*
> *the fragrance of the grass*
> *speaks to me.*
>
> *The summit of the mountain,*
> *the thunder of the sky,*
> *the rhythm of the sea,*
> *speaks to me. . . .*
>
> *And my heart soars.*[1]

These voices began to unfold a collective story. It is the story of women and men throughout history and prehistory seeking to align their spirit with the creative power that pervades the material world. It is the story of a common spiritual heritage we choose to call Earth Prayer. And it is based on one single recognition: we are, body and spirit, one with the Earth and with all of creation.

Over and over again, the prayers in this book remind us of this universal marriage of matter and spirit. They call on us to rethink the dualism of our culture that separates the sacred and the secular, the natural and the supernatural, body and mind. They make it clear that we humans are not here simply as transients waiting for a ticket to somewhere else. The Earth itself *is* Christos, *is* Buddha, *is* Allah, *is* Gaia.

In every religion we find the need to consecrate our participation in the natural world. This is especially evident in the tribal religions of native peoples. Their songs and prayers express a great courtesy toward the natural world. For example, the refrain "We return thanks" in the thanksgiving ritual of the Iroquois Indians—first to our mother, the Earth which sustains us, then to the rivers and streams, to the bushes and trees, to the elements, and finally to the Great Spirit who directs all things—reveals the intimacy of their relation with the entire Earth community.

A similar sensitivity can be found in many other cultures. Chang Tsai, an eleventh-century administrative official in China, placed this inscription on his office wall so that he would always have it before him:

> *Heaven is my father and earth my mother and even such a small creature as I finds an intimate place in its midst. That which extends throughout the universe, I regard as my body and that which directs the universe, I regard as my nature. All people are my brothers and sisters and all things are my companion.*

The Christian liturgical calendar, though primarily concerned with celebrating historical events in the life of Jesus, also links us to the cycles of the seasons. Its great Advent and Easter liturgies invite us to pause and enter into these sacred moments of the Earth's story. Likewise, the disciples of Buddha, without considering the necessity of formal prayers, have always wished well for all creation: "May all beings be happy." And this is the ultimate in Earth Prayer, whether we call it prayer or not.

In preparing this book we discovered that for many people today, it is not religious prayer at all, but poetry, that they turn to in their search for spiritual nourishment. Perhaps this is because so many conventional religious prayer books seem unable to consecrate the normal and the natural. Preoccupied with a world beyond this one, the revelatory power of the Earth goes unpraised.

Poetry, however, is unhampered by this dualism of sacred and profane and is more free to reach for wholeness. Its mythic images and evocative words expand our awareness, enabling us to experience ways of seeing, hearing, and feeling other than our own. Seeing and feeling with this degree of sensitivity enables the leap of consciousness into Earth Prayer. Consequently, this book draws from a great volume of world poetry.

> *Sometimes, when a bird cries out,*
> *Or the wind sweeps through a tree,*
> *Or a dog howls in a far off farm,*
> *I hold still and listen a long time.*

My world turns and goes back to the place
Where, a thousand forgotten years ago,
The bird and the blowing wind
Were like me, and were my brothers.

My soul turns into a tree,
And an animal, and a cloud bank.
Then changed and odd it comes home
And asks me questions. What should I reply?[2]

Over time we both came to see that the essence of Earth Prayer lies not so much in the words we use—be they poetic prayers or prayerful poems—as in the concentrated attention we give to it. The moment of prayer is always an event. Something happens. An intention offers itself; a moment of concentration and expressed vision. Like yoga or meditation, Earth Prayer is a way to collect the wandering faculties of the mind. Through prayerful concentration we sense how we are a "spoken" as well as a "speaking" reality: a receiver; a listener. We listen to the world around us and allow the impressions made upon us by the outer world, and the expressions of our inner life, to flow into one another, to enhance and reflect each other.

As we deepened our understanding of prayer, differences within the form became less important. The voices in this book address the "Lord," the "Great Spirit," "Wakan Tanka," "Goddess"—each acknowledging the spiritual precedents of their culture. Underlying these differences in salutation is the recognition that the transcendent is not separate from creation. The divine may be sacred, powerful, vulnerable, or fearsome, but it is always embodied and ultimately unnameable.

Earth Prayer is a tradition with particular meaning for our time. Faced as we are now with the diminishing richness and vitality of life on Earth, we need to understand and re-experience our unity with the natural world. Fostering this transformation is the challenge and task of our generation. The beauty of Earth Prayer is that it reminds us that we are not alone in this task. In forest clearings, beneath star-filled skies, in cathedrals, and before the hearth, men and women have always given voice to this impulse. In these prayers of the Earth we join our voice with theirs to call forth the healing that is so needed.

ELIZABETH ROBERTS
ELIAS AMIDON
COLORADO, 1990

---

[1] Chief Dan George
[2] Hermann Hesse

EARTH
PRAYERS

I

THE ECOLOGICAL
SELF

EARTH PRAYER BEGINS
with our intuition of the oneness of all life. We recognize that our
identity is inextricably entwined with lives beyond our own. This
sense of expanded identity goes beyond human relationships. We
depend upon trees, trees depend upon grasses, grasses depend
upon animals, mountains depend upon oceans, the dolphin de-
pends upon the farthest star. Physically and spiritually, we all are
woven into the living processes of the Earth. We take part in—as
science now tells us—a planet-sized living system. Our breathing,
our acting, our thinking arise in interaction with our shared world.
Our own hearts constantly beat out the cosmic rhythm within us.
We cannot escape our involvement any more than we can escape
breathing the air that has traveled from plants thousands of miles
away.

> *The mountains, I become part of it . . .*
> *The herbs, the fir tree, I become part of it.*
> *The morning mists, the clouds, the gathering*
>   *waters,*
> *I become part of it. . . .*[1]

When we ground our spiritual awareness in this ecological context, then the strength and wisdom of the living Earth, in all its manifestations, flows through us. Our Earth Prayer becomes a means of acting upon ourselves. It helps us to empty the self and to open our hearts to be filled with empathy and creativity.

The ecological self, like any notion of selfhood, is simply a metaphor, but it is a dynamic one. It involves our choice. We can choose at different moments to identify with different aspects of our interrelated existence—be they hunted whales, or homeless humans, or the planet itself. The prayers in this chapter remind us of this deep kinship—our bondedness with all of creation.

> *Look deeply: I arrive in every second*
> *to be a bud on a spring branch,*
> *to be a tiny bird, with wings still fragile,*
> > *learning to sing in my new nest,*
> *to be a caterpillar in the heart of a flower,*
> *to be a jewel hiding itself in a stone. . . .*
>
> *Please call me by my true names,*
> > *so I can wake up,*
> *and so the door of my heart can be left open,*
> *the door of compassion.*[2]

These prayers seek to heal the division that has grown between us and the rest of nature. They tell us: Pay attention. Attend to the relationships alive among all forms of life. Use imagination to explore the binding curve that joins us together. Seek to know the other. Join with it. Care for it as for yourself. When the human spirit is understood in this sense, as the mode of consciousness in which we are connected to the planet as a whole, it becomes clear that our entire life is an Earth Prayer.

[1] Navajo chant
[2] Thich Nhat Hanh

We are Nature, long have we been absent, but now we return,
We become plants, trunks, foliage, roots, bark,
We are bedded in the ground, we are rocks,
We are oaks, we grow in the openings side by side,
We browse, we are two among the wild herds, spontaneous as any,
We are two fishes swimming in the sea together,
We are what locust blossoms are, we drop scent around lanes
        mornings and evenings,
We are also the coarse smut of beasts, vegetables, minerals,
We are two predatory hawks, we soar above and look down,
We are two resplendent suns, we it is who balance ourselves
        orbic and stellar, we are as two comets,
We prowl fang'd and four-footed in the woods, we spring on prey,
We are two clouds forenoons and afternoons driving overhead,
We are seas mingling, we are two of those cheerful waves rolling
        over each other and interwetting each other,
We are what the atmosphere is, transparent, receptive, pervious,
        impervious,
We are snow, rain, cold, darkness, we are each product and
        influence of the globe,
We have circled and circled till we have arrived home again,
        we too,
We have voided all but freedom and all but our own joy.

WALT WHITMAN

The mountains, I become part of it . . .
The herbs, the fir tree, I become part of it.
The morning mists, the clouds, the gathering
        waters,
I become part of it.
The wilderness, the dew drops, the
        pollen . . .
I become part of it.

NAVAJO CHANT

I am the one whose praise echoes on high.
I adorn all the earth.
I am the breeze that nurtures all things green.
I encourage blossoms to flourish with ripening fruits.
I am led by the spirit to feed the purest streams.
I am the rain coming from the dew
that causes the grasses to laugh with the joy of life.
I am the yearning for good.

HILDEGARD OF BINGEN

5

It is lovely indeed, it is lovely indeed.

I, I am the spirit within the earth.
The feet of the earth are my feet;
The legs of the earth are my legs.
The strength of the earth is my strength;
The thoughts of the earth are my thoughts;
The voice of the earth is my voice.
The feather of the earth is my feather;
All that belongs to the earth belongs to me;
All that surrounds the earth surrounds me.
I, I am the sacred works of the earth.
It is lovely indeed, it is lovely indeed.

SUSANNE ANDERSON

Sometimes, when a bird cries out,
Or the wind sweeps through a tree,
Or a dog howls in a far-off farm,
I hold still and listen a long time.

My world turns and goes back to the place
Where, a thousand forgotten years ago,
The bird and the blowing wind
Were like me, and were my brothers.

My soul turns into a tree,
And an animal, and a cloud bank.
Then changed and odd it comes home
And asks me questions. What should I reply?

HERMANN HESSE

I am a feather on the bright sky
I am the blue horse that runs in the plain
I am the fish that rolls, shining, in the water
I am the shadow that follows a child
I am the evening light, the lustre of meadows
I am an eagle playing with the wind
I am a cluster of bright beads
I am the farthest star
I am the cold of the dawn
I am the roaring of the rain
I am the glitter on the crust of the snow
I am the long track of the moon in a lake
I am a flame of four colors
I am a deer standing away in the dusk
I am a field of sumac and the pomme blanche
I am an angle of geese in the winter sky
I am the hunger of a young wolf
I am the whole dream of these things

You see, I am alive, I am alive
I stand in good relation to the earth
I stand in good relation to the gods
I stand in good relation to all that is beautiful
I stand in good relation to all the daughters of Tsen-tainte
You see, I am alive, I am alive

N. SCOTT MOMADAY

I'm the mad cosmic
Stones plants mountains
Greet me Bee rats
Lions and eagles
Stars twilights dawns
Rivers and jungles all ask me
What's new How you doing?
And while stars and waves have something to say
It's through my mouth they'll say it

VICENTE HUIDOBRO

9

Teach your children
what we have taught our children—
that the earth is our mother.
Whatever befalls the earth
befalls the sons and daughters of the earth.
If men spit upon the ground,
they spit upon themselves.

This we know.
The earth does not belong to us;
we belong to the earth.
This we know.
All things are connected
like the blood which unites one family.
All things are connected.

Whatever befalls the earth
befalls the sons and daughters of the earth.
We did not weave the web of life;
We are merely a strand in it.
Whatever we do to the web,
we do to ourselves. . . .

CHIEF SEATTLE

Do not say that I'll depart tomorrow
because even today I still arrive.

Look deeply: I arrive in every second
to be a bud on a spring branch,
to be a tiny bird, with wings still fragile,
      learning to sing in my new nest,
to be a caterpillar in the heart of a flower,
to be a jewel hiding itself in a stone.

I still arrive, in order to laugh and to cry,
      in order to fear and to hope,
the rhythm of my heart is the birth and
      death of all that are alive.

I am the mayfly metamorphosing in the
      surface of the river,
and I am the bird which, when spring comes,
      arrives in time to eat the mayfly.

I am the frog swimming happily in the
      clear water of a pond,
and I am also the grass-snake who,
      approaching in silence,
      feeds itself on the frog.

I am the child in Uganda, all skin and bones,
　　　my legs as thin as bamboo sticks,
and I am the arms merchant, selling deadly
　　　weapons to Uganda.

I am the 12-year-old girl, refugee
　　　on a small boat,
who throws herself into the ocean after
　　　being raped by a sea pirate,
and I am the pirate, my heart not yet capable
　　　of seeing and loving.

I am a member of the politburo, with
　　　plenty of power in my hand,
and I am the man who has to pay his
　　　"debt of blood" to my people,
dying slowly in a forced labor camp.

My joy is like spring, so warm it makes
　　　flowers bloom in all walks of life.
My pain is like a river of tears, so full it
　　　fills up the four oceans.

Please call me by my true names,
so I can hear all my cries and my laughs
　　　at once,
so I can see that my joy and pain are one.

12

Please call me by my true names,
    so I can wake up,
and so the door of my heart can be left open,
the door of compassion.

THICH NHAT HANH

Earth mother, star mother,
You who are called by
        a thousand names,
May all remember
        we are cells in your body
        and dance together.
You are the grain
        and the loaf
That sustains us each day,
And as you are patient
        with our struggles to learn
So shall we be patient
        with ourselves and each other.
We are radiant light
        and sacred dark
        —the balance—
You are the embrace that heartens
And the freedom beyond fear.
Within you we are born
        we grow, live, and die—
You bring us around the circle
        to rebirth,
Within us you dance
Forever.

STARHAWK

I was born part of this earth.
My Grandmother Earth.
I was born part of this earth.
My Mother, all living beings.
I was born part of this earth.
My Grandfather, the sky.
I was born part of this earth.
My Father, all creatures of the air.
I was born part of this earth.
The eight Grandfathers.
I was born part of the earth.
The four corners of the earth.
I was born part of this earth.
The great wind giant of the North.
I was born part of this earth.
The red road of the dead.
I was born part of this earth.
The blue and black road of destruction.
I was born part of this earth.
The old ones say
the old way's gone,
the old ones say.
Still,
I was born part of this earth.

DANIEL WESTERN

We live by the sun
We feel by the moon
We move by the stars

We live in all things
All things live in us

We eat from the earth
We drink from the rain
We breathe of the air

We live in all things
All things live in us

We call to each other
We listen to each other
Our hearts deepen with love and compassion

We live in all things
All things live in us

We depend on the trees and animals
We depend on the earth
Our minds open with wisdom and insight

We live in all things
All things live in us

We dedicate our practice to others
We include all forms of life
We celebrate the joy of living-dying

We live in all things
All things live in us

We are full of life
We are full of death
We are grateful for all beings and companions

STEPHANIE KAZA, GREEN GULCH FARM

Black people, we rainclouds

closer to the sun and full of life
soaking up the knowledge of the earth
                          and
storing it within ourselves
                  moving on
to spread truth throughout the world

we black clouds.
loved and feared.
ready to explode and give new life
to a dying planet

beautiful dark clouds
casting shadows of blackness
shadows of dignity
shadows of
                    love

giving of ourselves to promote life
                    while
realizing our ability to destroy

rainclouds

                    we are

nature
nature
nature

natural!!!
black people, we rainclouds

closer to the sun and full of life

MARVIN WYCHE, JR.

Birds nest in my arms,
on my shoulders, behind my knees,
between my breasts there are quails,
they must think I'm a tree.
The swans think I'm a fountain,
they all come down and drink when I talk.
When sheep pass, they pass over me,
and perched on my fingers, the sparrows eat,
the ants think I'm the earth,
and men think I'm nothing.

GLORIA FUERTES

The great sea has set me in motion.
Set me adrift,
And I move as a weed in the river.

The arch of sky
And mightiness of storms
Encompasses me,
And I am left
Trembling with joy.

ESKIMO SONG

Clouds are flowing in the river, waves are flying in the sky.
Life is laughing in a pebble. Does a pebble ever die?

Flowers grow out of the garbage, such a miracle to see.
What seems dead and what seems dying makes for butterflies
to be.

Life is laughing in a pebble, flowers bathe in morning dew.
Dust is dancing in my footsteps and I wonder who is who.

Clouds are flowing in the river, clouds are drifting in my tea,
On a never-ending journey, what a miracle to be!

EVELINE BEUMKES

The force that through the green fuse drives the flower
Drives my green age; that blasts the roots of trees
Is my destroyer.
And I am dumb to tell the crooked rose
My youth is bent by the same wintry fever.

The force that drives the water through the rocks
Drives my red blood; that dries the mouthing streams
Turns mine to wax.
And I am dumb to mouth unto my veins
How at the mountain spring the same mouth sucks.

The hand that whirls the water in the pool
Stirs the quick sand; that ropes the blowing wind
Hauls my shroud sail.
And I am dumb to tell the hanging man
How of my clay is made the hangman's lime . . .

DYLAN THOMAS

The man whose mind is rounded out to perfection
Knows full well
Truth is not cut in half
And things do not exist apart from the mind.

In the great Assembly of the Lotus all are present
Without divisions.
Grass, trees, the soil on which these grow
All have the same kinds of atoms.
Some are barely in motion
While others make haste along the path, but they
        will all in time
Reach the Precious Island of Nirvana
Who can really maintain
That things inanimate lack buddhahood?

CHAN-JAN

We know ourselves to be made from this earth. We know this earth is made from our bodies. For we see ourselves. And we are nature. We are nature seeing nature. We are nature with a concept of nature. Nature weeping. Nature speaking of nature to nature.

The red-winged blackbird flies in us, in our inner sight. We see the arc of her flight. We measure the ellipse. We predict its climax. We are amazed. We are moved. We fly. We watch her wings negotiate the wind, the substance of the air, its elements and the elements of those elements, and count those elements found in other beings, the sea urchin's sting, ink, this paper, our bones, the flesh of our tongues with which we make the sound "blackbird," the ear with which we hear, the eye which travels the arc of her flight. And yet the blackbird does not fly in us but in somewhere else free of our minds, and now even free of our sight, flying in the path of her own will.

SUSAN GRIFFIN

Tent tethered among jackpine and blue-
bells. Lacewings rise from rock
incubators. Wild geese flying north.
And I can't remember who I'm supposed
to be.

I want to learn how to purr. Abandon
myself, have mistresses in maidenhair
fern, own no tomorrow nor yesterday:
a blank shimmering space forward and
back. I want to think with my belly.
I want to name all the stars animals
flowers birds rocks in order to forget
them, start over again. I want to
wear the seasons, harlequin, become
ancient and etched by weather. I
want to be snow pulse, ruminating
ungulate, pebble at the bottom of the
abyss, candle burning darkness rather
than flame. I want to peer at things

shameless, observe the unfastening,
that stripping of shape by dusk.
I want to sit in the meadow a rotten
stump pungent with slimemold, home
for pupae and grubs, concentric rings
collapsing into the passacaglia of
time. I want to crawl inside someone
and hibernate one entire night with
no clocks to wake me, thighs fragrant
loam. I want to melt. I want to swim
naked with an otter. I want to turn
insideout, exchange nuclei with the
Sun. Toward the mythic kingdom of
summer I want to make blind motion,
using my ribs as a raft, following
the spiders as they set sail on their
tasselled shining silk. Sometimes
even a single feather's enough
to fly.

ROBERT MACLEAN

27

I am of the family of the universe, and with all of us together I do not fear being alone; I can reach out and touch a rock or a hand or dip my feet in water. Always there is some body close by, and when I speak I am answered by a plane's roar or the bird's whistling or the voices of others in conversation far apart from me. When I lie down to sleep, I am in the company of the dark and the stars.

Breathe to me, sheep in the meadow. Sun and moon, my father and my father's brother, kiss me on the brow with your light. My sister, earth, holds me up to be kissed. Sun and moon, I smile at you both and spread my arms in affection and lay myself down at full length for the earth to know I love it too and am never to be separated from it. In no way shall death part us.

DAVID IGNATOW

Those who are dead are never gone:
They are there in the thickening shadow.
The dead are not under the earth:
they are in the tree that rustles,
they are in the wood that groans,
they are in the water that sleeps,
they are in the hut, they are in the crowd,
the dead are not dead.

Those who are dead are never gone,
they are in the breast of the woman,
they are in the child who is wailing
and in the firebrand that flames.
The dead are not under the earth:
they are in the fire that is dying,
they are in the grasses that weep,
they are in the whimpering rocks,
they are in the forest, they are in the house,
the dead are not dead.

BIRAGO DIOP

Do not stand at my grave and weep
I am not there. I do not sleep.

I am a thousand winds that blow.
I am the diamond glint on snow.

I am the sunlight on ripened grain.
I am the gentle autumn rain.

When you wake in the morning hush
I am the swift, uplifting rush
of quiet birds in circling flight.
I am the soft starlight at night.

Do not stand at my grave
and weep.
I am not there. I do not sleep.

JOYCE FOSSEN

A long time I have lived with you
And now we must be going
Separately to be together.
Perhaps I shall be the wind
To blur your smooth waters
So that you do not see your face too much.
Perhaps I shall be the star
To guide your uncertain wings
So that you have direction in the night.
Perhaps I shall be the fire
To separate your thoughts
So that you do not give up.
Perhaps I shall be the rain
To open up the earth
So that your seed may fall.
Perhaps I shall be the snow
To let your blossoms sleep
So that you may bloom in spring.
Perhaps I shall be the stream
To play a song on the rock
So that you are not alone.
Perhaps I shall be a new mountain
So that you always have a home.

NANCY WOOD

31

Now Talking God
With your feet I walk
I walk with your limbs
I carry forth your body
For me your mind thinks
Your voice speaks for me
Beauty is before me
And beauty is behind me
Above and below me hovers the beautiful
I am surrounded by it
I am immersed in it
In my youth I am aware of it
And in old age I shall walk quietly
The beautiful trail.

NATIVE AMERICAN PRAYER

Don't Grieve.
Anything you lose comes around in another form.
The child weaned from mother's milk
now drinks wine and honey mixed.
God's joy moves from unmarked box to unmarked box,
from cell to cell.
As rainwater,
down into flowerbed.
As roses, up from ground.
Now it looks like a plate of rice and fish,
Now a cliff covered with vines,
Now a horse being saddled.
It hides within these,
till one day it cracks them open.

. . . Fa'ilatun, fa'ilatun, fa'ilatun fa'ilat
There's the light gold of wheat in the sun,
and the gold of bread made from wheat . . .
I have neither, I am only talking about them

as a town in the desert looks up
to stars on a clear night.

RUMI

We call upon the spirit of evolution, the miraculous force that inspires rocks and dust to weave themselves into biology. You have stood by us for millions and billions of years—do not forsake us now. Empower us and awaken in us pure and dazzling creativity. You that can turn scales into feathers, seawater to blood, caterpillars to butterflies, metamorphose our species, awaken in us the powers that we need to survive the present crisis and evolve into more aeons of our solar journey.

Awaken in us a sense of who we truly are: tiny ephemeral blossoms on the Tree of Life. Make the purposes and destiny of that tree our own purpose and destiny.

Fill each of us with love for our true Self, which includes all of the creatures and plants and landscapes of the world. Fill us with a powerful urge for the wellbeing and continual unfolding of this Self.

May we speak in all human councils on behalf of the animals and plants and landscapes of the Earth.

May we shine with a pure inner passion that will spread rapidly through these leaden times.

May we all awaken to our true and only nature—none other than the nature of Gaia, this living planet Earth.

We call upon the power which sustains the planets in their orbits, that wheels our Milky Way in its 200-million-year spiral, to imbue our personalities and our relationships with harmony, endurance and joy. Fill us with a sense of immense time so that our brief, flickering lives may truly reflect the work of vast ages past and also the millions of years of evolution whose potential lies in our trembling hands.

O stars, lend us your burning passion.
O silence, give weight to our voice.
We ask for the presence of the spirit of Gaia.

JOHN SEED

II

A SACRED
PLACE

To THE ANCIENTS, AS
well as to many contemporary seekers, the world is alive with spirit.
The surrounding landscape is infused with creativity and meaning
and each place speaks to us of the divine.

> *Every day is a god, each day is a god*
> *and holiness holds forth in time. . . .*[1]

This notion of a richly sacralized world may seem strange to the
mainstream western culture. We live in a secular landscape. We
have been taught to identify the sacred primarily with cathedrals,
churches, and temples. The rest of the Earth is considered real
estate—a mere "it" to be used as a resource for our benefit. This
effort to desacralize the world, dispel its sacred aura, is what made
possible our commercial relationship to the land. It has allowed us
to plunder the natural world, destroying places of more power and
beauty than we will ever be able to recreate.

The poems and prayers in this section encourage us to reacquaint
ourselves with the immanence of the spirit in the natural world.
They are filled with a deep love of the Earth and awe in the
presence of its mystery. They remind us that every notion we have

of the spirit has been shaped by our experience of this Earth. If we have a wonderful sense of the divine it is because we live amid such awesome magnificence. As the Passionist priest Thomas Berry observes, "If we lived on the moon, our mind and emotions, our speech, our imagination, our sense of the divine would all reflect the desolation of the lunar landscape." Clearly the Earth is our primary revelatory environment. Our most sacred scripture is the "holy book" of Nature.

> It is written on the arched sky;
> It looks out from every star . . .
> It is spread out like a legible language upon the
>   broad face of an unsleeping ocean.
> It is the poetry of Nature;
> It is that which uplifts the spirit within us . . .[2]

While the distinction between spirit and matter is valid, no one can separate the two; no one can draw a line between them. Spirit and matter are not two different realms of reality, two different layers of the universe. One and the same reality will be material or spiritual depending on how we approach it. No matter where we immerse ourselves in the stream of reality, we can touch the spiritual source of all that is natural.

From this perspective the Earth is a bountiful community of living beings of which we are only one part. And each living being has an inner presence and dignity apart from any value we humans may place upon it. While certain places always have been recognized for the powerful presence of their unique localities or landforms, these places are not isolated entities. All the physical things that make up our daily life share a common spiritual reality—as such they are all to be revered and respected.

[1] Annie Dillard
[2] John Ruskin

Lord, the air smells good today, straight from the mysteries
within the inner courts of God.
A grace like new clothes thrown
across the garden, free medicine for everybody.
The trees in their prayer, the birds in praise,
the first blue violets kneeling.
Whatever came from Being is caught up in being, drunkenly
forgetting the way back.

RUMI

Every day is a god, each day is a god,
and holiness holds forth in time.
I worship each god,
I praise each day splintered down,
and wrapped in time like a husk,
a husk of many colors spreading,
at dawn fast over the mountains split.

ANNIE DILLARD

And I thought over again
My small adventures
As with a shore-wind I drifted out
In my kayak
And thought I was in danger,

My fears,
Those small ones
That I thought so big
For all the vital things
I had to get and to reach.

And yet, there is only
One great thing,
The only thing:
To live to see in huts and on journeys
The great day that dawns,
And the light that fills the world.

INUIT SONG

The beauty of the trees,
the softness of the air,
the fragrance of the grass,
     speaks to me.

The summit of the mountain,
the thunder of the sky,
the rhythm of the sea,
     speaks to me.

The faintness of the stars,
the freshness of the morning,
the dewdrop on the flower,
     speaks to me.

The strength of fire,
the taste of salmon,
the trail of the sun,
and the life that never goes away,
     they speak to me.

And my heart soars.

CHIEF DAN GEORGE

Ah to be alive
    on a mid-September morn
    fording a stream
    barefoot, pants rolled up
    holding boots, pack on,
    sunshine, ice in the shallows,
    northern rockies.

Rustle and shimmer of icy creek waters
stones turn underfoot, small and hard on toes
    cold nose dripping
    singing inside
    creek music, heart music,
    smell of sun on gravel.

    I pledge allegiance.

I pledge allegiance to the soil
    of Turtle Island
    one ecosystem
    in diversity
    under the sun—
With joyful interpenetration for all.

GARY SNYDER

43

You should entreat trees and rocks
to preach the Dharma, and you
should ask rice fields and gardens
for the truth. Ask pillars for the
Dharma and learn from hedges
and walls. Long ago the great god
Indra honored a wild fox as his
own master and sought the
Dharma from him, calling him
"Great Bodhisattva."

EIHEI DOGEN

I part the out thrusting branches
and come in beneath
the blessed and the blessing trees.
Though I am silent
there is singing around me.
Though I am dark
there is vision around me.
Though I am heavy
there is flight around me.

WENDELL BERRY

44

the sun
she
is setting
in the tall grass
beneath the pines

where the heart
beats
one with the land

where the mule deer
approach
their antlers raised

where with palms
upturned
we pray

CHARLIE MEHRHOFF

The earth is at the same time
mother,
she is mother of all that is natural,
mother of all that is human,
She is the mother of all,
for contained in her
are the seeds of all.

The earth of humankind
contains all moistness,
all verdancy,
all germinating power.

It is in so many ways
fruitful.
All creation comes from it.
Yet it forms not only the basic
raw material for humankind,
but also the substance
of the incarnation
of God's son.

HILDEGARD OF BINGEN

For the Lord your God
is bringing you
into a good land,

a land
of flowing streams,
with springs and underground waters
welling up in valleys and hills,
a land of wheat and barley,
of vines and fig trees and pomegranates,
a land of olive trees and honey,
a land where you may eat bread without
        scarcity,
where you will lack nothing,
a land whose stones are iron
and from whose hills you may mine copper.

You shall eat your fill
and bless the Lord your God
for the good land
he has given you.

DEUTERONOMY 8:7–11, NRSV

tall
lush
rain
forest
dripping in the morning
wild orchids banana flowers
thick vines drape los palos del sol & great white cedar;
Others w/ five foot green elephant ears flopping,
hundreds of butterflies, orange caterpillars, blue
        mosquitos, pink mushrooms,
& industrious leaf cutting ants commuting w/ hunks of
        green to store in infinite
ant caverns & nourish among the fungus formed
        therein;
tiny crimson roots twist around larger roots twisting
        around thicker branches spiraling around
larger trunks of trees, disneyesque the organic
        biospheric plumbing in the world

& a black butterfly w/ red striped wings flutters
        without a sound
through the billions of green leaves quivering moist in
        the patchy sunlight

JOSEPH RICHEY

You ask
why I perch
on a jade green mountain?
I laugh
but say nothing
my heart
free
like a peach blossom
in the flowing stream
going by
in the depths
in another world
not among men

LI PO

O beautiful for spacious skies,
For amber waves of grain;
For purple mountains' majesty,
Above the fruited plain.
America, America,
God shed his grace on thee,
And crown thy good with brotherhood
From sea to shining sea.

KATHERINE LEE BATES

Blessed is the spot, and the house,
        and the place, and the city,
                and the heart, and the mountain,
    and the refuge, and the cave,
            and the valley, and the land,
                and the sea, and the island,
    and the meadow where mention
        of God hath been made,
                and His praise glorified.

BAHÁ'Í PRAYER BY BAHA 'U' LLA'H

Although they have tightly bound my arms and legs,
All over the mountain I hear the song of birds,
And the forest is filled
with the perfume of spring-flowers.
Who can prevent me from freely enjoying these,
Which take from the long journey
a little of its loneliness?

HO CHI MINH

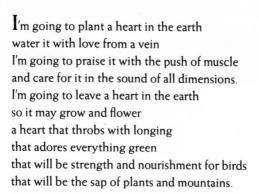

I'm going to plant a heart in the earth
water it with love from a vein
I'm going to praise it with the push of muscle
and care for it in the sound of all dimensions.
I'm going to leave a heart in the earth
so it may grow and flower
a heart that throbs with longing
that adores everything green
that will be strength and nourishment for birds
that will be the sap of plants and mountains.

ROSARIO MURILLO

51

The Earth,
adorned with heights and gentle slopes and plains,
bears plants and herbs of various healing powers.
May she spread wide for us, afford us joy!

On whom are ocean, river, and all waters,
on whom have sprung up food and ploughman's crops,
on whom moves all that breathes and stirs abroad—
Earth, may she grant to us the long first draught!

Whatever I dig up of you, O Earth,
may you have quick replenishment!
O purifying One, may my thrust never
reach right into your vital points, your heart!

O Earth, O Mother, dispose my lot
in gracious fashion that I may be at ease,
and in harmony with your powers.

ATHARVA VEDA XII

O God, my mother, my father, lord of the
hills, lord of the valleys, lord of the
forest, be patient with me. I am about to
do what has always been done.

Now I make you an offering, that you may be
warned: I am about to molest your
heart. Perhaps you will have the
strength to endure it.

I am going to work you in order that I may
live.

Let no animal pursue me, no snake, no
scorpion, no wasp annoy me, no falling
timber hit me, no ax, no machete catch
me.

With all my heart I am going to work you.

KEKCHI MAYA,
PRAYER BEFORE CLEARING A FIELD

Consider the life of trees.
Aside from the axe, what trees acquire from man is inconsiderable.
What man may acquire from trees is immeasurable.
From their mute forms there flows a poise, in silence;
a lovely sound and motion in response to wind.
What peace comes to those aware of the voice and bearing of
    trees!
Trees do not scream for attention.
A tree, a rock, has no pretence, only a real growth out of itself,
in close communion with the universal spirit.
A tree retains a deep serenity.
It establishes in the earth not only its root system but also
those roots of its beauty and its unknown consciousness.
Sometimes one may sense a glisten of that consciousness, and with
such perspective, feel that man is not necessarily the highest
form of life.

CEDRIC WRIGHT

The way we stand, you can see we have grown up this way together, out of the same soil, with the same rains, leaning in the same way toward the sun. See how we lean together in the same direction. How the dead limbs of one of us rest in the branches of another. How those branches have grown around the limbs. How the two are inseparable. And if you look you can see the different ways we have taken this place into us. Magnolia, loblolly bay, sweet gum, Southern bayberry, Pacific bayberry; wherever we grow there are many of us; Monterey pine, sugar pine, white-bark pine, four-leaf pine, single-leaf pine, bristle-cone pine, foxtail pine, Torrey pine, Western red pine, Jeffrey pine, bishop pine.

And we are various, and amazing in our variety, and our differences multiply, so that edge after edge of the endlessness of possibility is exposed. You know we have grown this way for years. And to no purpose you can understand. Yet what you fail to know we know, and the knowing is in us, how we have grown this way, why these years were not one of them heedless, why we are shaped the way we are, not all straight to your purpose, but to ours. And how we are each purpose, how each cell, how light and soil are in us, how we are in the soil, how we are in the air, how we are both infinitesimal and great and how we are infinitely without any purpose you can see, in the way we stand, each alone, yet none of us separable, none of us beautiful when separate but all exquisite as we stand, each moment heeded in this cycle, no detail unlovely.

SUSAN GRIFFIN

There is religion in everything around us,
A calm and holy religion
In the unbreathing things in Nature.
It is a meek and blessed influence,
Stealing in as it were unaware upon the heart;
It comes quickly, and without excitement;
It has no terror, no gloom;
It does not rouse up the passions;
It is untrammelled by creeds . . .
It is written on the arched sky;
It looks out from every star;
It is on the sailing cloud and in the invisible wind;
It is among the hills and valleys of the earth
Where the shrubless mountain-top pierces the thin atmosphere
        of eternal winter,
Or where the mighty forest fluctuates before the strong wind,
With its dark waves of green foliage;
It is spread out like a legible language upon the broad face of
        an unsleeping ocean;
It is the poetry of Nature;
It is that which uplifts the spirit within us . . .
And which opens to our imagination a world of spiritual beauty
        and holiness.

JOHN RUSKIN

How wonderful, O Lord, are the works of your hands!
The heavens declare Your glory,
the arch of sky displays Your handiwork.
In Your love You have given us the power
to behold the beauty of Your world
robed in all its splendor.
The sun and the stars, the valleys and hills,
the rivers and lakes all disclose Your presence.
The roaring breakers of the sea tell of Your awesome might;
the beasts of the field and the birds of the air
bespeak Your wondrous will.
In Your goodness You have made us able to hear
the music of the world. The voices of loved ones
reveal to us that You are in our midst.
A divine voice sings through all creation.

JEWISH PRAYER

In protecting the earth, we found good pine needles and harsh
    dried wood along with rocks helpful.
When you begin to examine our earth,
You find tiny mushrooms and small grass blades,
Ornamented by the chatter of ground squirrels.
You find our soil is soft and rocky;
It does not permit artificial soil topping.
Our pine trees are diligent, dedicated and graceful;
In either life or death they will always perform their duty of
    pinetreeness,
Equipped with sap and bark.
We find our world of wilderness so refreshing.
Along with summer's drum, we produce occasional
    thundershowers, wet and dry messages:
We can't miss the point,
Since this earth is so bending and open to us, along with the
    rocks,
We are not shy,
We are so proud—
We can make a wound in a pine tree and it bleeds sap, and courts
    us, in spite of the setting-sun shadow;
They bend and serve so graciously, whether dead or alive.
We love our pines and rocks;
They are not covered with the superstitious setting-sun chemical
    manure of this and that.

We are so proud of the sky that we produce on our horizon.
Our stars twinkle and wink as if they know us;
We have no problem of recognition.
Our rocks and pine trees speak for us.

C. T. MUKPO

O Lord, Thou art on the sandbanks
As well as in the midst of the current;
I bow to Thee.
Thou art in the little pebbles
As well as in the calm expanse of the sea;
I bow to Thee.
O all-pervading Lord,
Thou art in the barren soil
And in crowded places;
I bow to Thee.

'SUKLA YAJUR, VEDA XVI

I believe the earth
exists, and
in each minim mote
of its dust the holy
glow of thy candle.
Thou
unknown I know,
thou spirit,
giver,
lover of making, of the
wrought letter,
wrought flower,
iron, deed, dream.
Dust of the earth,
help thou my
unbelief. Drift,
gray become gold, in the beam of
vision. I believe with
doubt. I doubt and
interrupt my doubt with belief. Be,
beloved, threatened world.
      Each minim
mote.
      Not the poisonous
luminescence forced

out of its privacy,
the sacred lock of its cell
broken. No,
the ordinary glow
of common dust in ancient sunlight.
Be, that I may believe. Amen.

DENISE LEVERTOV

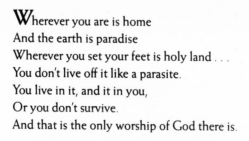

Wherever you are is home
And the earth is paradise
Wherever you set your feet is holy land . . .
You don't live off it like a parasite.
You live in it, and it in you,
Or you don't survive.
And that is the only worship of God there is.

WILFRED PELLETIER AND TED POOLE

61

And God saw everything that He had made, and found it very
   good."
And He said: This is a beautiful world that I have given you.
Take good care of it; do not ruin it.
It is said: Before the world was created, the Holy One kept
creating worlds and destroying them. Finally He created this one,
and was satisfied. He said to Adam: This is the last world I
shall make. I place it in your hands: hold it in trust.

JEWISH PRAYER

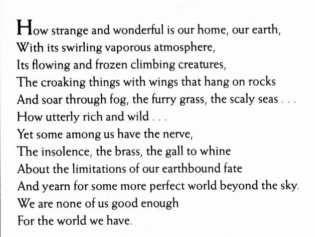

How strange and wonderful is our home, our earth,
With its swirling vaporous atmosphere,
Its flowing and frozen climbing creatures,
The croaking things with wings that hang on rocks
And soar through fog, the furry grass, the scaly seas . . .
How utterly rich and wild . . .
Yet some among us have the nerve,
The insolence, the brass, the gall to whine
About the limitations of our earthbound fate
And yearn for some more perfect world beyond the sky.
We are none of us good enough
For the world we have.

EDWARD ABBEY

Few things that grow here poison us.
Most of the animals are small.
Those big enough to kill us do it in a way
Easy to understand, easy to defend against.
The air, here, is just what the blood needs.
We don't use helmets or special suits.

The Star, here, doesn't burn you if you
Stay outside as much as you should.
The worst of our winters is bearable.
Water, both salt and sweet, is everywhere.
The things that live in it are easily gathered.
Mostly, you can eat them raw with safety and pleasure.

Yesterday my wife and I brought back
Shells, driftwood, stones, and other curiosities
Found on the beach of the immense
Fresh-water Sea we live by.
She was all excited by a slender white stone which:
"Exactly fits the hand!"

I couldn't share her wonder:
Here, almost everything does.

LEW WELCH

63

III

THE PASSION
OF THE EARTH

IN THIS SECTION OF
Earth Prayers the pain of the Earth is expressed. Knowing that the
world is an intricate balance of parts we see that if one of the parts
is sick or wounded, its plight and suffering affects us all. Here we
humble ourselves before all creation and allow the outcries of despair from around the globe to touch our hearts, opened by the
realization of an ecological self.

Today the ability of the Earth to support life is being deeply
eroded. The evidence is everywhere. We are mindlessly destroying
the very web of life; millions of people are dying each year as a
result of direct ecological collapse. Within the animal and plant
kingdoms we are witnessing the greatest holocaust in history. Millions of species are on the verge of extinction. The old forests are
being felled, the top soil washed away, and the groundwater con-
taminated. The air is polluted and the rain is acid. So the litany
goes on, as every aspect of life on the planet is profoundly altered
by the way our culture has organized the business of its existence.

They've lost it, lost it,
and their children

will never even wish for it—
and I am afraid . . .
because the sun keeps rising
and these days
nobody sings.[1]

While many of us are aware of the destruction taking place on our planet, it is difficult to integrate this knowledge into our daily life. What do we do when it is not war that is killing us, but progress? When the problem is not the actions of an evil "other," but ourselves? We fear the despair such information provokes. We don't want to feel the grief over all that is lost, nor our own complicity in the damage. This denial of feeling takes a heavy toll on us, impoverishing our sensory and emotional life. Ultimately, it puts us out of touch with reality.

There is a historical tradition of prayer that foresees the ruination of the world because of human transgression. We find it in the Old Testament, we find it again in the prayers of Native Americans as they witness the destruction of their way of life by the European conquerors. We are hearing it again now, as citizens from around the world express their fears and their grief at what is happening to the Earth.

We have forgotten who we are.

We have sought only our own security
We have exploited simply for our own ends
We have distorted our knowledge
We have abused our power.[2]

---

[1]Aaron Kramer
[2]U.N. Environmental Sabbath Program

The earth dries up and withers,
    the world languishes and
        withers,
    the heavens languish together
        with the earth.
The earth lies polluted
    under its inhabitants;
for they have transgressed laws,
    violated the statutes,
        broken the everlasting covenant.

ISAIAH 24:4–5, NRSV

They've lost it, lost it,
and their children
will never even wish for it—
and I am afraid
that the whole tribe's in trouble,
the whole tribe is lost—
because the sun keeps rising
and these days
nobody sings.

AARON KRAMER

68

The high,
the low
all of creation,
God gives to humankind to use. If this privilege is misused,
God's Justice permits creation to punish humanity.

HILDEGARD OF BINGEN

We who prayed and wept
for liberty from kings
and the yoke of liberty
accept the tyranny of things
we do not need.
In plenitude too free,
we have become adept
beneath the yoke of greed.

Those who will not learn
in plenty to keep their place
must learn it by their need
when they have had their way
and the fields spurn their seed.
We have failed Thy grace.
Lord, I flinch and pray,
send Thy necessity.

WENDELL BERRY

We have forgotten who we are.

We have forgotten who we are
We have alienated ourselves from the unfolding
    of the cosmos
We have become estranged from the movements
    of the earth
We have turned our backs on the cycles of life.

We have forgotten who we are.

We have sought only our own security
We have exploited simply for our own ends
We have distorted our knowledge
We have abused our power.

We have forgotten who we are.

Now the land is barren
And the waters are poisoned
And the air is polluted.

We have forgotten who we are.

Now the forests are dying
And the creatures are disappearing
And humans are despairing.

We have forgotten who we are.

We ask forgiveness
We ask for the gift of remembering
We ask for the strength to change.

We have forgotten who we are.

U.N. ENVIRONMENTAL SABBATH PROGRAM

Sausalito,
   Little Willow.
Perfect Beach by the last Bay in the world.
   None more beautiful.

Today we kneel at thy feet
   And curse the men who have misused you.

LEW WELCH

Too much industry
too much eats
too much beer
too much cigarettes

Too much philosophy
too many thought forms
not enough rooms—
not enough trees

Too much Police
too much computers
too much hi fi
too much Pork

Too much coffee
too much smoking
under slate grey roofs
Too much obedience

Too many bellies
Too many business suits
Too much paperwork
too many magazines

Too much industry
No fish in the Rhine

Lorelei poisoned
Too much embarrassment

Too many fatigued
workers on the train
Ghost Jews scream
on the streetcorner

Too much old murder
too much white torture
Too much one Stammheim
too many happy Nazis

Too many crazy students
Not enough farms
not enough Appletrees
Not enough nut trees

Too much money
Too many poor
turks without vote
"Guests" do the work

Too much metal
Too much fat
Too many jokes
not enough meditation . . .

ALLEN GINSBERG

Long ago
the ancients say
this land was free
and we shared it all
with the mountains and the sea
the birds and the trees
we lived in peace
long ago
before those others came
and built fences
by cutting the trees
dug mines
by cutting the earth
removed her blood
the oil that lies within
formed long ago
like us
who lived in peace

the birds sang less
without the trees
the land became dry
without the birds

to plant the flowers
and we too became quiet
watching our mountains die
listening for the birds
that no longer flew—
but still we lived in peace

what sustained us
through all those years?
the nights of silence
and the songs of the frogs

for we know
as the ancients said
this land will again be free
and we will again share it all
with the mountains and the sea
the birds and the trees
for·we still live in peace
and we wish you the same
for we are all one

HARRIET KOFALK, INSPIRED BY THE BRIBRI,
INDIGENOUS COSTA RICANS

Spirit of love
That flows against our flesh
Sets it trembling
Moves across it as across grass
Erasing every boundary that we
accept
And swings the doors of our lives
wide—
This is a prayer I sing:
Save our perishing earth!

Spirit that cracks our
single selves—
Eyes fall down eyes,
Hearts escape through the bars
        of
our ribs
To dart into other bodies—
Save this earth!
The earth is perishing.
This is a prayer I sing.

Spirit that hears each one of us,
Hears all that is—
Listens, listens, hears us out—
Inspire us now!
Our own pulse beats in every
stranger's throat,
And also there within the flowered
ground beneath
    our feet,
And—teach us to listen!—
We can hear it in water, in wood,
and even in stone.
We are earth of this earth, and we
are bone of its bone.
This is a prayer I sing, for we have
forgotten this
    and so
The earth is perishing.

BARBARA DEMING

Don't destroy the world.
I've only nibbled
the grasses of my lover's meadow.
We are early May
and clematis has not yet blossomed.
Alyssum, lady's slipper, buttercups
I want to hold them to her chin as we did childhood summers
shining their yellow reflection.

And the large magnificent trees
rhododendron, splashed pink as dawn
magnolia, white waxy bowls of purple swooning.
I've waited my lifetime for this.
Plums are yet to come, fat, taut
the fragile bloom misting their skin like breath.

Let there be days of grainy juices
sticky on my face. I
want time. There's

plush mango I smear over her.
Let me lick the pit clean, memorize
each crevice with my tongue.

Don't
destroy
the world
because my child's five, because
she cries when she scrapes her knee on gravel
    skin shredded, blood beading through the dust
cries pitifully and long
while I envision scenes of devastation:
    holding her against the clawing pain
    her screams, my helplessness.

"I hope nothing really bad ever happens to you," I blurt
the accusation, a shield for my own hysteria . . .

Don't. Don't destroy the world.

ELLEN BASS

Something will have gone out of us as
a people if we ever let the remaining
wilderness be destroyed; if we permit
the last virgin forests to be turned into
comic books and plastic cigarette
cases; if we drive the few remaining
members of the wild species into zoos
or to extinction; if we pollute the last
clear air and dirty the last clean streams
and push our paved roads through the
last of the silence, so that never again
will Americans be free in their own
country from the noise, the exhausts,
the stinks of human and automotive
waste. And so that never again can we
have the chance to see ourselves single,
separate, vertical and individual in the
world, part of the environment of trees
and rocks and soil, brother to the other
animals, part of the natural world and
competent to belong in it.

WALLACE STEGNER

Imagine a place without a pipeline,
Without an oil well,
Without a rig.
Imagine a place without a coal pit,
Without a smoke stack,
Acid rain free.

Imagine a land of long white vistas,
Ice cold saviours,
Gleaming glaciers,
Breaking into the sea.
Imagine the Earth without an oil slick,
Free of pollution,
No radioactivity.

Imagine a place on Earth so awesome,
So vast so pure,
We can hardly breathe its air.
Imagine the Earth alive with morning,
Shimmering white nights,
No end of sky,
No end of sea.

CAROLE FORMAN, "ANTARCTICA"

Great Spirit, whose dry lands thirst, help us to find
the way to refresh your lands.

We pray for your power to refresh your lands.

Great Spirit, whose waters are choked with debris and
pollution, help us to find the way to cleanse your waters.

We pray for your knowledge to find the way to cleanse the waters.

Great Spirit, whose beautiful earth grows ugly with
misuse, help us to find the way to restore beauty to your
handiwork.

We pray for your strength to restore the beauty of your
handiwork.

Great Spirit, whose creatures are being destroyed,
help us to find a way to replenish them.

We pray for your power to replenish the earth.

Great Spirit, whose gifts to us are being lost in
selfishness and corruption, help us to find the way
to restore our humanity.

We pray for your wisdom to find the way to restore our humanity.

U.N. ENVIRONMENTAL SABBATH PROGRAM

Infinite Spirit, when I pray each day
for shelter for the homeless,
let me not ignore the pet without a home;

As I ask protection for those in areas
of turmoil and unrest,
let me not forget endangered species of life;

When I pray that the hungry be fed,
let me be mindful
that all God's creatures have need of sustenance;

As I ask Divine assistance for those afflicted
by fire, flood, earthquake, storm or drought,
let me remember that this includes every living thing;

In seeking miracle cures for human disease,
may I also speak for the well-being of the planet itself.

Let the words of my mouth,
the meditations of my heart
and the actions of my life be as one,
that I may live each day in harmony
with Mother Earth. Amen.

JENNIE FROST BUTLER

Here we are, God—a planet at prayer. Attune our spirits
that we may hear your harmonies and bow before your creative
     power
that we may face our violent discords and join with your Energy
to make heard in every heart your hymn of peace.

Here we are, God—a militarized planet. Transform our fears
that we may transform our war fields into wheatfields, arms
into handshakes, missiles into messengers of peace.

Here we are, God—a polluted planet. Purify our vision that
we may perceive ways to purify our beloved lands, cleanse our
precious waters, de-smog our life-giving air.

Here we are, God—an exploited planet. Heal our heart, that
we may respect our resources, hold priceless our people, and
provide for our starving children an abundance of daily bread.

JOAN METZNER

Lord, make this world to last as long as possible.

PRAYER OF AN ELEVEN-YEAR-OLD CHILD,
ON HEARING OF SINO-INDIAN BORDER FIGHTING

Who

took the dream
of the land

who staked down "private property"
through the soul of the deer

who
diverted streams
cleared forests
burned fields

i
seek to know
my own name

i
seek to know
why

after all that i have done
to hurt her
does the Mother continue
to embrace me

CHARLIE MEHRHOFF

Hey! Lean to hear my feeble voice.
>   At the center of the sacred hoop
>   You have said that I should make the tree to bloom.
With tears running, O Great Spirit, my
Grandfather,
>   With running eyes I must say
>   The tree has never bloomed
Here I stand, and the tree is withered.
>   Again, I recall the great vision you gave me.
It may be that some little root of the sacred tree still lives.
>   Nourish it then
>   That it may leaf
>   And bloom
>   And fill with singing birds!
Hear me, that the people may once again
>   Find the good road
>   And the shielding tree.

BLACK ELK

When the animals come to us,
    asking for our help,
    will we know what they are saying?

When the plants speak to us
    in their delicate, beautiful language,
    will we be able to answer them?

When the planet herself
    sings to us in our dreams,
    will we be able to wake ourselves, and act?

GARY LAWLESS

IV

HEALING THE WHOLE

DURING THIS TIME OF
great imbalance on planet Earth we may feel ourselves torn between the priorities of healing ourselves—resolving our own inner
spiritual or psychological problems—and attempting to cure the
social and economic ills that beset our culture. While each of us
undoubtedly has much inner work to do, this attitude misses the
main point of Earth Prayer. It continues to view the individual as
somehow separate from the rest of the world. But if we accept that
we are totally part of this living Earth, then we must recognize that
isolated health is an illusion. Healing ourselves and working to re-
solve the contradictions in the human-Earth ecology is the same
work.

All healing involves making whole again—resolving the contradictions that exist between self and other, body and spirit, mind and
nature. The prayers in this section show us a pathway back to an
understanding and appreciation of life. They remind us that our
participation extends to the whole. Knowing that we are not encap-
sulated, self-enclosed entities, but rather fields of energy integrated
with the environment, everything we do transforms and reshapes
the world. If our actions can destroy, so can they heal. In this light

there is no difference between work and prayer, no distinction between physical activity and the work of the spirit. Precisely in the restoration of this balance between body and spirit lies the path for healing the greater whole.

> *You do not have to be good.*
> *You do not have to walk on your knees*
> *for a hundred miles through the desert repenting.*
> *You only have to let the soft animal of your body*
> *love what it loves. . . .*[1]

The voices in the following pages remind us that the Earth is itself the primary healer. They speak of silence and solitude. They tell us of the comfort to be found in wild places. As Nancy Wood writes, "My help is in the mountains / Where I take myself to heal / the earthly wounds / That people give to me. . . ."

Finally, these prayers remind us that what we would like to see, we must help bring into being. All prayer is ultimately an act of hope. Without hope it has no substance. Hope empowers our intention and gives character to our action. While our action may be turned aside from its purpose or taken over by the milieu in which it occurs, prayer, when it is genuine, cannot be taken over. It attains its goals because it is its goal.

I have come to terms with the future.
From this day onward I will walk
easy on the earth. Plant trees. Kill
no living things. Live in harmony with
all creatures. I will restore
the earth where I am. Use no more
of its resources than I need. And listen,
listen to what it is telling me.[2]

---

[1]Mary Oliver
[2]M. J. Slim Hooey

We who have lost our sense and our senses—our touch, our smell, our vision of who we are; we who frantically force and press all things, without rest for body or spirit, hurting our earth and injuring ourselves: we call a halt.

We want to rest. We need to rest and allow the earth to rest. We need to reflect and to rediscover the mystery that lives in us, that is the ground of every unique expression of life, the source of the fascination that calls all things to communion.

We declare a Sabbath, a space of quiet: for simply being and letting be; for recovering the great, forgotten truths; for learning how to live again.

U.N. ENVIRONMENTAL SABBATH PROGRAM

Let us be united;
Let us speak in harmony;
Let our minds apprehend alike.
Common be our prayer;
Common be the end of our assembly;
Common be our resolution;
Common be our deliberations.
Alike be our feelings;
Unified be our hearts;
Common be our intentions;
Perfect be our unity.

FROM THE RIG VEDA

We join with the earth and with each other.

To bring new life to the land
To restore the waters
To refresh the air

We join with the earth and with each other.

To renew the forests
To care for the plants
To protect the creatures

We join with the earth and with each other.

To celebrate the seas
To rejoice in the sunlight
To sing the song of the stars

We join with the earth and with each other.

To recreate the human community
To promote justice and peace
To remember our children

We join with the earth and with each other.

We join together as many and diverse expressions
    of one loving mystery: for the healing of the
    earth and the renewal of all life.

U.N. ENVIRONMENTAL SABBATH PROGRAM

Grandfather,
Look at our brokenness.

We know that in all creation
Only the human family
Has strayed from the Sacred Way.

We know that we are the ones
Who are divided
And we are the ones
Who must come back together
To walk in the Sacred Way.

Grandfather,
Sacred One,
Teach us love, compassion, and honor
That we may heal the earth
And heal each other.

OJIBWAY PRAYER

Let us think of Mother Earth, her rich bounty that will result from springtime, the golden corn and the seeds of harvest, all grown strong from Mother Earth, the spring rains, and the energy of Father Sky. It is time to consider healing: healing of ourselves, healing of a loved one, healing of adversaries for peace among nations, and healing of the harms done to Mother Earth.

> Oh, Great Spirit,
> I pray for myself in order that I may be healed.
> Oh, Great Spirit,
> I pray for my close friend who is sick and needs help.
> Oh, Great Spirit,
> I pray for this world so that all these atomic weapons
> And other bad things that we point at each other
> Will someday soon all be destroyed.
> I pray that adversaries will communicate
> And all of the mistrust will be healed.
> Oh, Great Spirit,
> I pray for the environment.
> I pray for its cleansing
> And the renewal of our Mother Earth.

> ED McGAA, EAGLE MAN

My help is in the mountain
Where I take myself to heal
The earthly wounds
That people give to me.
I find a rock with sun on it
And a stream where the water runs gentle
And the trees which one by one give me company.
So must I stay for a long time
Until I have grown from the rock
And the stream is running through me
And I cannot tell myself from one tall tree.
Then I know that nothing touches me
Nor makes me run away.
My help is in the mountain
That I take away with me.

Earth cure me. Earth receive my woe. Rock
strengthen me. Rock receive my weakness. Rain
wash my sadness away. Rain receive my doubt.
Sun make sweet my song. Sun receive the anger
from my heart.

NANCY WOOD

Blessed sister, holy mother, spirit of the fountain,
    spirit of the garden,
Suffer us not to mock ourselves with falsehood
Teach us to care and not to care
Teach us to sit still
Even among these rocks.
Our peace in his will
And even among these rocks
Sister, mother,
And spirit of the river, spirit of the sea.
Suffer me not to be separated
And let my cry come unto Thee.

T.S. ELIOT

I swear the earth shall surely be complete to him or
her who shall be complete,
The earth remains jagged and broken only to him
or her who remains jagged and broken.

I swear there is no greatness or power that does not
emulate those of the earth,
There can be no theory of any account unless it
corroborate the theory of the earth,
No politics, song, religion, behavior, or what not,
is of account, unless it compare with the
amplitude of the earth,
Unless it face the exactness, vitality, impartiality,
rectitude of the earth.

WALT WHITMAN

You do not have to be good.
You do not have to walk on your knees
for a hundred miles through the desert, repenting.
You only have to let the soft animal of your body
love what it loves.
Tell me about despair, yours, and I will tell you mine.
Meanwhile the world goes on.
Meanwhile the sun and the clear pebbles of the rain
are moving across the landscapes,
over the prairies and the deep trees,
the mountains and the rivers.
Meanwhile the wild geese, high in the clean blue air,
are heading home again.
Whoever you are, no matter how lonely,
the world offers itself to your imagination,
calls to you like the wild geese, harsh and exciting—
over and over announcing your place
in the family of things.

MARY OLIVER

When we get out of the glass bottles of our ego,
and when we escape like squirrels turning in the
      cages of our personality
and get into the forests again,
we shall shiver with cold and fright
but things will happen to us
so that we don't know ourselves.

Cool, unlying life will rush in,
and passion will make our bodies taut with power,
we shall stamp our feet with new power
and old things will fall down,
we shall laugh, and institutions will curl up like
      burnt paper.

D. H. LAWRENCE

When despair for the world grows in me
and I wake in the night at the least sound
in fear of what my life and my children's lives may be,
I go and lie down where the wood drake
rests in his beauty on the water, and the great heron feeds.
I come into the peace of wild things
who do not tax their lives with forethought
of grief. I come into the presence of still water.
And I feel above me the day-blind stars
waiting with their light. For a time
I rest in the grace of the world, and am free.

WENDELL BERRY

Tired of all who come with words, words but no language
I went to the snow-covered island.
The wild does not have words.
The unwritten pages spread themselves out in all directions!
I come across the marks of roe-deer's hooves in the snow.
Language but no words.

TOMAS TRANSTROMER

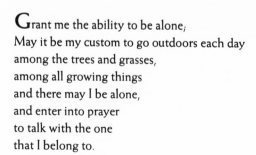

First you must love your body, in games
in wild places, in bodies of others,
Then you must enter the world of men and
learn all worldly ways. You must sicken.
You must return to your Mother and notice
how quiet the house is.
Then return to the world that is
not Man
that you may finally walk in the
world of Man, speaking.

LEW WELCH

Grant me the ability to be alone;
May it be my custom to go outdoors each day
among the trees and grasses,
among all growing things
and there may I be alone,
and enter into prayer
to talk with the one
that I belong to.

RABBI NACHMAN OF BRATZLAV

103

A little too abstract, a little too wise,
It is time for us to kiss the earth again,
It is time to let the leaves rain from the skies,
Let the rich life run to the roots again.
I will go down to the lovely Sur Rivers
And dip my arms in them up to the shoulders.
I will find my accounting where the alder leaf quivers,
In the ocean wind over the river boulders.
I will touch things and things and no more thoughts,
That breed like mouthless May-flies darkening the sky,
The insect clouds that blind our passionate hawks
So that they cannot strike, hardly can fly.
Things are the hawk's food and noble is the mountain,
    Oh noble
Pico Blanco, steep sea-wave of marble.

ROBINSON JEFFERS

Let the trees be consulted
before you take any action
every time you breathe in
thank a tree
let treeroots crack parking lots
at the world bank headquarters
let loggers be druids
specially trained and rewarded
to sacrifice trees at auspicious times
let carpenters be master artisans
let lumber be treasured like gold
let chainsaws be played like saxophones
let soldiers on maneuvers plant trees
give police and criminals
a shovel and a thousand seedlings
let businessmen carry pocketfuls of acorns
let newlyweds honeymoon in the woods
walk don't drive
stop reading newspapers
stop writing poetry
squat under a tree
and tell stories

JOHN WRIGHT

We call upon the earth, our planet home, with its beautiful
    depths and soaring heights, its vitality and abundance of life,
    and together we ask that it:

Teach us, and show us the way.

We call upon the mountains, the Cascades and the Olympics, the
    high green valleys and meadows filled with wild flowers, the
    snows that never melt, the summits of intense silence, and we
    ask that they:

Teach us, and show us the way.

We call upon the waters that rim the earth, horizon to horizon,
    that flow in our rivers and streams, that fall upon our gardens
    and fields, and we ask that they:

Teach us, and show us the way.

We call upon the land which grows our food, the nurturing soil,
    the fertile fields, the abundant gardens and orchards, and we
    ask that they:

Teach us, and show us the way.

We call upon the forests, the great trees reaching strongly to the
    sky with earth in their roots and the heavens in their
    branches, the fir and the pine and the cedar, and we ask
    them to:

106   Teach us, and show us the way.

We call upon the creatures of the fields and forests and the seas, our brothers and sisters the wolves and deer, the eagle and dove, the great whales and the dolphin, the beautiful Orca and salmon who share our Northwest home, and we ask them to:

Teach us, and show us the way.

We call upon all those who have lived on this earth, our ancestors and our friends, who dreamed the best for future generations, and upon whose lives our lives are built, and with thanksgiving, we call upon them to:

Teach us, and show us the way.

And lastly, we call upon all that we hold most sacred, the presence and power of the Great Spirit of love and truth which flows through all the universe . . . to be with us to:

Teach us, and show us the way.

CHINOOK BLESSING LITANY

To live content with small means,
to seek elegance rather than luxury,
and refinement rather than fashion,
to be worthy, not respectable, and wealthy, not rich,
to study hard, think quietly, talk gently, act frankly,
to listen to stars and birds, babes and sages, with open heart,
to bear all cheerfully,
do all bravely,
await occasions,
hurry never—
in a word, to let the spiritual, unbidden and unconscious,
grow up through the common.
This is to be my symphony.

WILLIAM ELLERY CHANNING

I have come to terms with the future.
From this day onward I will walk
easy on the earth. Plant trees. Kill
no living things. Live in harmony with
all creatures. I will restore the earth
where I am. Use no more of its resources
than I need. And listen, listen to what
it is telling me.

M.J. SLIM HOOEY

Let there be peace, welfare and righteousness
in every part of the world.

Let confidence and friendship prevail
for the good of east and west
for the good of the needy south
for the good of all humanity.

Let the people inspire their leaders
helping them to seek peace by peaceful means
helping them and urging them
to build a better world
a world with a home for everybody
a world with food and work for everybody
a world with spiritual freedom
for everybody.

Let those who have the power of money
be motivated by selfless compassion.
Let money become a tool
for the good of humankind.

Let those who have power
deal respectfully with the resources of the planet.
Let them respect and maintain
the purity of the air, water, land and subsoil.
Let them co-operate to restore
the ecological soundness of Mother Earth.

Let trees grow up by the billions
around the world.
Let green life invade the deserts.

Let industry serve humanity
and produce waste that serves nature.

Let technology respect
the holiness of Mother Earth.

Let those who control the mass media
contribute to create mutual understanding
contribute to create optimism and confidence.

Let ordinary people
meet by the millions across the borders.
Let them create a universal network
of love and friendship.

Let billions of human beings
co-operate to create a good future
for their children and grandchildren.

Let us survive
In peace and harmony with Mother Earth.

HAGEN HASSELBALCH

It is up to us to receive and transmit our Torah.
It is up to us to see that the world still stands.
May the time be not distant
when nation will not lift up sword against nation,
neither shall they learn war any more.
They shall beat their swords into ploughshares,
for the earth will be filled with the wonder of life.
Then shall we sit under our vine and our fig tree
and none shall be afraid.

RABBI RAMI M. SHAPIRO

We seek a renewed stirring of life for the earth
We plead that what we are capable of doing is
not always what we ought to do.
We urge that all people now determine
that a wide untrammeled freedom shall remain
to testify that this generation has love for the next.
If we want to succeed in that, we might show, meanwhile,
a little more love for this one, and for each other.

NANCY NEWHALL

From that which we fear, make us fearless.
O bounteous One, assist us with your aid.

May the atmosphere we breathe
breathe fearlessness into us:
fearlessness on earth
and fearlessness in heaven!
May fearlessness surround us
above and below!

May we be without fear
by night and by day!
    Let all the world be my friend!

          ATHARVA VEDA XIX

                ꙳

Brothers of the sea,
Look at the stars,
Look at the deep blue
And set the world free.
Our right is to live and be free;
Freedom will not come from outside.
It is only in ourselves united.

     SAMAR FISHERMEN'S SONG, PHILIPPINES

Almighty God, who are mother and father to us all,
Look upon your planet Earth divided:
Help us to know that we are all your children;
That all nations belong to one great family,
And all of our religions lead to you.

Multiply our prayers in every land
Until the whole Earth becomes your congregation,
United in your love.
Sustain our vision of a peaceful future
And give us strength to work unceasingly
To make that vision real. Amen.

HELEN WEAVER

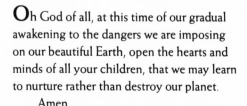

Oh God of all, at this time of our gradual
awakening to the dangers we are imposing
on our beautiful Earth, open the hearts and
minds of all your children, that we may learn
to nurture rather than destroy our planet.
    Amen.

LORRAINE R. SCHMITZ

115

House made of dawn.
House made of evening light.
House made of the dark cloud.
House made of male rain.
House made of dark mist.
House made of female rain.
House made of pollen.
House made of grasshoppers.

Dark cloud is at the door.
The trail out of it is dark cloud.
The zigzag lightning stands high upon it.
An offering I make.
Restore my feet for me.
Restore my legs for me.
Restore my body for me.
Restore my mind for me.
Restore my voice for me.
This very day take out your spell for me.

Happily I recover.
Happily my interior becomes cool.

Happily I go forth.
My interior feeling cool, may I walk.
No longer sore, may I walk.
Impervious to pain, may I walk.
With lively feelings may I walk.
As it used to be long ago, may I walk.

Happily may I walk.
Happily, with abundant dark clouds, may I walk.
Happily, with abundant showers, may I walk.
Happily, with abundant plants, may I walk.
Happily, on a trail of pollen, may I walk.
Happily may I walk.
Being as it used to be long ago, may I walk.

May it be beautiful before me.
May it be beautiful behind me.
May it be beautiful below me.
May it be beautiful above me.
May it be beautiful all around me.
In beauty it is finished.
In beauty it is finished.

NAVAJO CHANT

Great Spirit,
give us hearts to understand;
never to take
from creation's beauty more than we give;
never to destroy wantonly for the furtherance of
      greed;
never to deny to give our hands for the building of
      earth's beauty;
never to take from her what we cannot use.
Give us hearts to understand that to destroy earth's
      music is to create confusion;
that to wreck her appearance is to blind us to beauty;
that to callously pollute her fragrance is to make a
      house of stench;
that as we care for her she will care for us. Amen.

U.N. ENVIRONMENTAL SABBATH PROGRAM

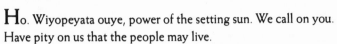

Ho. Wiyopeyata ouye, power of the setting sun. We call on you. Have pity on us that the people may live.

Wakinyan, thunder beings of the black west, we call on you. You are the source of both the power to live and of destruction, who ride the back of minne wichoni, the life-giving rains.

For long years, the way of the people has been weak and there has been fear. Many have said that the red road would disappear and that the six powers and Wakan Tanka would turn their faces from us.

It is true that many of the old ways have been lost. But just as the life-giving rains restore the earth after the drought, so your power will restore the Way and give it new life.

We ask this not only for the red people but for all the people that they might live. In ignorance and carelessness they have walked upon Ina Maka, our Mother. They did not understand that they are part of all beings, the four-legged, the winged, grandfather rock, the tree people, and our star brothers. Now the earth and all our relations are crying out. They cry for the help of all people.

ED McGAA, EAGLE MAN

Knowing how deeply our lives intertwine,
  We vow not to kill.

Knowing how deeply our lives intertwine,
  We vow to not take what is not given.

Knowing how deeply our lives intertwine,
  We vow to not engage in abusive relationships.

Knowing how deeply our lives intertwine,
  We vow to not speak falsely or deceptively.

Knowing how deeply our lives intertwine,
  We vow to not harm self or others through poisonous
  thought or substance.

Knowing how deeply our lives intertwine,
    We vow to not dwell on past errors.

Knowing how deeply our lives intertwine,
    We vow to not speak of self separate from others.

Knowing how deeply our lives intertwine,
    We vow to not possess any thing or form of life selfishly.

Knowing how deeply our lives intertwine,
    We vow to not harbor ill will toward any plant, animal, or
    human being.

Knowing how deeply our lives intertwine,
    We vow to not abuse the great truth of the Three Treasures.

STEPHANIE KAZA, GREEN GULCH FARM

. . . So, friends, every day do something
that won't compute. Love the Lord.
Love the world. Work for nothing.
Take all that you have and be poor.
Love someone who does not deserve it.
Denounce the government and embrace
the flag. Hope to live in that free
republic for which it stands.
Give your approval to all you cannot
understand. Praise ignorance, for what man
has not encountered he has not destroyed.
Ask the questions that have no answers.
Invest in the millennium. Plant sequoias.
Say that your main crop is the forest
that you did not plant,
that you will not live to harvest.
Say that the leaves are harvested
when they have rotted into the mold.
Call that profit. Prophesy such returns.
Put your faith in the two inches of humus
that will build under the trees
every thousand years.
Listen to carrion—put your ear
close, and hear the faint chattering

of the songs that are to come.
Expect the end of the world. Laugh.
Laughter is immeasurable. Be joyful
though you have considered all the facts.
So long as women do not go cheap
for power, please women more than men.
Ask yourself: Will this satisfy
a woman satisfied to bear a child?
Will this disturb the sleep
of a woman near to giving birth?
Go with your love to the fields.
Lie easy in the shade. Rest your head
in her lap. Swear allegiance
to what is nighest your thoughts.
As soon as the generals and the politicos
can predict the motions of your mind,
lose it. Leave it as a sign
to mark the false trail, the way
you didn't go. Be like the fox
who makes more tracks than necessary,
some in the wrong direction.
Practice resurrection.

WENDELL BERRY

Hear, O Humankind, the prayer of my heart

For are we not one, have we not one desire,
to heal our Mother Earth and bind her wounds
to hear again from dark forests and flashing rivers
the varied ever-changing Song of Creation?

O humankind, are we not all brothers and sisters,
are we not the grandchildren of the Great Mystery?
Do we not all want to love and be loved, to work
and to play, to sing and dance together?

But we live with fear. Fear that is hate, fear
that is mistrust, envy, greed, vanity, fear that is
ambition, competition, aggression, fear that is
loneliness, anger, bitterness, cruelty . . . and yet,
fear is only twisted love, love turned back on itself,
love that was denied, love that was rejected . . .
and love . . .

  Love is life—creation, seed and leaf
and blossom and fruit and seed, love is growth
and search and reach and touch and dance.
Love is nurture and succor and feed and pleasure,

love is pleasuring ourselves pleasuring each other,
love is life believing in itself.
    And life . . .
Life is the Sacred Mystery singing to itself, dancing
to its drum, telling tales, improvising, playing
and we are all that Spirit, our stories all
but one cosmic story that we are love indeed,
that perfect love in me seeks the love in you,
and if our eyes could ever meet without fear
we would recognize each other and rejoice,
for love is life believing in itself.

                MANITONGQUAT

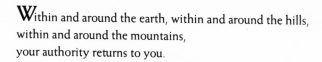

Within and around the earth, within and around the hills,
within and around the mountains,
your authority returns to you.

             ALFONSO ORTIZ

V

THE
ELEMENTS

FOR TENS OF THOUSANDS of years cultures developed in close attunement with the elemental energies of the cosmos. The Chinese recognized five primal elements: Fire, Earth, Metal, Water, and Wood. Native Americans included Sacred Sound while the ancient Greeks identified the four energies of Earth, Air, Water, and Fire. These weren't simply ideas or metaphors. Their power was experienced as real. Rivers, mountains, fire, hurricanes, lightning all spoke of the grandeur of the universe and the importance of living in right relation with these elemental forces. To stay in touch with this power, it was common to celebrate or pray to these basic elements of life.

> *My words are tied in one*
> *With the great mountains,*
> *With the great rocks,*
> *With the great trees,*
> *In one with my body*
> *And my heart.*[1]

The prayers and poems of this section remind us of our roots. We are made of the planet's elemental energies: Water—"washing and nourishing through endless riverways of gut and vein and capillary"; Earth—pouring "through us, replacing each cell in the body every seven years"; Air—its "oxygen kissing each cell awake"; Fire—"from our sun that fuels all life."

Yet as basic as these elemental energies are to our own lives, it is easy in the modern world to dissociate ourselves from them. Our search for comfort and security and our fear of Nature's forces has led us to use our technology to create a barrier between ourselves and the natural world. We tend to forget that when the wind blows coolly on our face we are feeling the generosity of the universe or that sunlight on our arms is the touch of the great cosmic flame. It is easy to lose our place in Earth's story.

It is time to regain our mythic respect for these cosmic dynamics and to open our lives to the blessings of Earth, Air, Fire, and Water. These are the elemental cycles that underlie all evolution. Our future and that of our children lies not in overcoming them but in aligning ourselves with their energies.

Ancient sun, eternally young,
giver of life and source of energy,
　　In coal and oil, in plant and wind and tide,
　　in spiritual light and human embrace,
You kindle the heavens, you shine within us
(for we are suns with hearts afire—
　　we light the world as you light the sky
　　and find clouds within whose shadows are dark),
We give thanks for your rays. . . .[2]

[1]Yokuts Indian prayer
[2]Congregation of Abraxas

What are you? What am I? Intersecting cycles of water, earth, air and fire, that's what I am, that's what you are.

Water—blood, lymph, mucus, sweat, tears, inner oceans tugged by the moon, tides within and tides without. Streaming fluids floating our cells, washing and nourishing through endless riverways of gut and vein and capillary. Moisture pouring in and through and out of you, of me, in the vast poem of the hydrological cycle. You are that. I am that.

Earth—matter made from rock and soil. It too is pulled by the moon as the magma circulates through the planet heart and roots suck molecules into biology. Earth pours through us, replacing each cell in the body every seven years. Ashes to ashes, dust to dust, we ingest, incorporate and excrete the earth, are made from the earth. I am that. You are that.

Air—the gaseous realm, the atmosphere, the planet's membrane. The inhale and the exhale. Breathing out carbon dioxide to the trees and breathing in their fresh exudations. Oxygen kissing each cell awake, atoms dancing in orderly metabolism, interpenetrating. That dance of the air cycle, breathing the universe in and out again, is what you are, is what I am.

Fire—fire from our sun that fuels all life, drawing up plants and raising the waters to the sky to fall again replenishing. The inner furnace of your metabolism burns with the fire of the Big Bang that first sent matter-energy spinning through space and

time. And the same fire as the lightning that flashed into the primordial soup catalyzing the birth of organic life.

You were there, I was there, for each cell of our bodies is descended in an unbroken chain from that event.

JOHN SEED AND JOANNA MACY

Sons and daughters of the earth, steep yourself in the sea of matter, bathe in its fiery waters, for it is the source of your life and your youthfulness.

You thought you could do without it because the power of thought has been kindled in you? You hoped that the more thoroughly you rejected the tangible, the closer you would be to spirit: that you would be more divine if you lived in the world of pure thought, or at least more angelic if you fled the corporeal? Well, you were like to have perished of hunger.

You must have oil for your limbs, blood for your veins, water for your soul, the world of reality for your intellect: do you not see that the very law of your own nature makes these a necessity for you?

PIERRE TEILHARD DE CHARDIN

The small plot of ground
on which you were born
cannot be expected

to stay forever
the same.
Earth changes,
and home becomes different
places.

You took flesh
from clay
but the clay
did not come
from just one
place.

To feel alive,
important, and safe,
know your own waters
and hills, but know
more.

You have stars in your bones
and oceans
in blood.

You have opposing
terrain in each eye.
You belong to the land
and sky of your first cry,
you belong to infinity.

ALLA RENEE BOZARTH

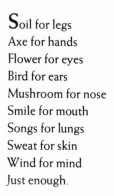

Soil for legs
Axe for hands
Flower for eyes
Bird for ears
Mushroom for nose
Smile for mouth
Songs for lungs
Sweat for skin
Wind for mind
Just enough.

NANAO SAKAKI

133

O Great Spirit of the East,
Radiance of the rising Sun,
Spirit of new beginnings,
O Grandfather Fire,
Great nuclear fire—of the Sun.
Power of life-energy, vital spark,
Power to see far, and to
Imagine with boldness.
Power to purify our senses,
Our hearts and our minds.

We pray that we may be aligned with You,
So that your powers may flow through us,
And be expressed by us,
For the good of this planet Earth,
And all living beings upon it.

O Great Spirit of the West,
Spirit of the Great Waters,
Of rain, rivers, lakes and springs.
O Grandmother Ocean,
Deep matrix, womb of all life.

Power to dissolve boundaries,
To release holdings,
Power to taste and to feel,
To cleanse and to heal,
Great blissful darkness of peace.

We pray that we may be aligned with You,
So that your powers may flow through us,
And be expressed by us,
For the good of this planet Earth,
And all living beings on it.

O Great Spirit of the North,
Invisible Spirit of the Air,
And of the fresh, cool winds,
O vast and boundless Grandfather Sky,
Your living breath animates all life.
Yours is the power of clarity and strength,
Power to hear the inner sounds,
To sweep out the old patterns,
And to bring change and challenge,
The ecstasy of movement and the dance.

We pray that we may be aligned with You,
So that your powers may flow through us,
And be expressed by us,
For the good of this planet Earth,
And all living beings on it.

O Great Spirit of the South,
Protector of the fruitful land,
And of all green and growing things,
The noble trees and grasses,
Grandmother Earth, Soul of Nature.
Great power of the receptive,
Of nurturance and endurance,
Power to grow and bring forth
Flowers of the field,
Fruits of the garden.

We pray that we may be aligned with You,
So that your powers may flow through us,
For the good of this planet Earth,
And all living beings upon it.

RALPH METZNER

O our mother the earth, O our father the sky,
Your children are we, and with tired backs
We bring you gifts that you love.
Then weave for us a garment of brightness;
May the warp be the white light of morning,
May the weft be the red light of evening,
May the fringes be the falling rain,
May the border be the standing rainbow.
Thus weave for us a garment of brightness
That we may walk fittingly where grass is green,
O our mother the earth, O our father the sky!

TEWA PUEBLO PRAYER

137

Blessed be the Wind!

Without wind, most of Earth would be uninhabitable. The tropics would grow so unbearably hot that nothing could live there, and the rest of the planet would freeze. Moisture, if any existed, would be confined to the oceans, and all but the fringe of the great continents . . . would be desert. There would be no erosion, no soil, and for any community that managed to evolve despite these rigors, no relief from suffocation by their own waste products.

But with the wind, Earth comes truly alive. Winds provide the circulatory and nervous systems of the planet, sharing out energy and information, distributing both warmth and awareness, making something out of nothing.

All wind's properties are borrowed. Our knowledge of it comes at secondhand, but it comes strongly. And this combination of a force that cannot be apprehended, but nevertheless has an undeniable existence, was our first experience of the spiritual. A crack in the cosmos that widened to let the tide of consciousness flow through.

We are the fruits of the wind—and have been seeded, irrigated, and cultivated by its craft.

LYALL WATSON

The day we die
the wind comes down
to take away
our footprints.

The wind makes dust
to cover up
the marks we left
while walking.

For otherwise
the thing would seem
as if we were
still living.

Therefore the wind
is he who comes
to blow away
our footprints.

SOUTHERN BUSHMEN

Ancient sun, eternally young,
giver of life and source of energy,
 In coal and oil, in plant and wind and tide,
 in spiritual light and human embrace,
You kindle the heavens, you shine within us
(for we are suns with hearts afire—
 we light the world as you light the sky
 and find clouds within whose shadows are dark);
We give thanks for your rays, and clouds your rays draw up,
for the sky route you travel faithfully as we traverse this globe,
 For our journeys of earth which draw us together,
 for our journeys of dream which sustain us when apart.
Ancient of Days, you rule the nations,
our birth and death: our journeys you have wrought.
 Loam we become for your fertile spirit.
 Your cosmic light penetrates our depths;
 In your majesty we are bound to one another.
We gather this morning as did people of old
with joys and woes, varied gifts and diverse needs.
 We offer you these in thanksgiving for life
 and share them through your generations on earth.

CONGREGATION OF ABRAXAS

Cattle browse peacefully
Trees and plants are verdant,
Birds fly from their nests
And lift up their wings in your praise.
All animals frisk upon their feet
All winged things fly and alight once more—
They come to life with your rising.

Boats sail upstream and boats sail downstream,
At your coming every highway is opened.
Before your face the fish leap up from the river,
Your rays reach the green ocean.
You it is who place the male seed in woman,
Who create the semen in man;
You quicken the sun in his mother's belly,
Soothing him so that he shall not cry.
Even in the womb you are his nurse.
You give breath to all your creation,
Opening the mouth of the newborn
And giving him nourishment.

FROM THE PHARAOH AKHENATEN'S
"HYMN TO THE SUN"

I've known rivers:
I've known rivers ancient as the world and older than the
    flow of human blood in human veins.

My soul has grown deep like the rivers.

I bathed in the Euphrates when dawns were young.
I built my hut near the Congo and it lulled me to sleep.
I looked upon the Nile and raised the pyramids above it.
I heard the singing of the Mississippi when Abe Lincoln
    went down to New Orleans, and I've seen its muddy
    bosom turn all golden in the sunset.

I've known rivers:
Ancient, dusky rivers.

My soul has grown deep like the rivers.

              LANGSTON HUGHES

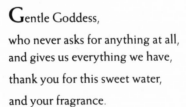

Gentle Goddess,

    who never asks for anything at all,
    and gives us everything we have,

    thank you for this sweet water,

    and your fragrance.

              LEW WELCH

Water.
Lakes and rivers.
Oceans and streams.
Springs, pools and gullies.
Arroyos, creeks, watersheds.
Pacific. Atlantic. Mediterranean.
Indian. Caribbean. China Sea.
(Lying. Dreaming on shallow shores.)
Arctic. Antarctic. Baltic.
Mississippi. Amazon. Columbia. Nile.
Thames. Sacramento. Snake. (Undulant woman river.)
Seine. Rio Grande. Willamette. McKenzie. Ohio.
Hudson. Po. Rhine. Rhone.
Rain. After a lifetime of drought.
That finally cleanses the air.
The soot from our eyes.
The dingy windows of our western home.
The rooftops and branches. The wings of birds.
The new light on a slant. Pouring. Making everything new.

PAULA GUNN ALLEN

To see the greatness of a mountain, one must keep one's distance;
To understand its form, one must move around it;
To experience its moods, one must see it at sunrise and sunset,
At noon and at midnight, in sun and in rain,
In snow and in storm, in summer and in winter
And in all the other seasons
He who can see the mountain like this comes near to the life of
    the mountain.

Mountains grow and decay, they breathe and pulsate with life.
They attract and collect invisible energies from their surroundings
The forces of the air, of the water, of electricity and magnetism;
They create winds, clouds, thunderstorms, rains, waterfalls
And rivers. They fill their surroundings with active life and give
    shelter and food to innumerable beings. Such is the greatness
    of mighty mountains.

LAMA GOVINDA

Why climb a mountain?

Look! a mountain there.

I don't climb mountain.
Mountain climbs me.

Mountain is myself.
I climb on myself.

There is no mountain
        nor myself.
        Something
        moves up and down
        in the air.

NANAO SAKAKI

My words are tied in one
With the great mountains,
With the great rocks,
With the great trees,
In one with my body
And my heart.

Do you all help me
With supernatural power,
And you, Day
And you, Night!
All of you see me
One with this world!

YOKUTS INDIAN PRAYER

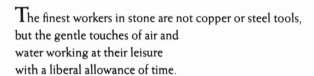

The finest workers in stone are not copper or steel tools,
but the gentle touches of air and
water working at their leisure
with a liberal allowance of time.

HENRY DAVID THOREAU

146

Listen to the air.
You can hear it, feel it,
smell it, taste it.
Woniya wakan, the holy air,
which renews all by its breath.
Woniya wakan, spirit, life, breath, renewal,
it means all that.
We sit together, don't touch,
but something is there,
we feel it between us,
as a presence.
A good way to start thinking about nature,
talk about it.
Rather talk to it,
talk to the rivers, to the lakes,
to the winds,
as to our relatives.

JOHN LAME DEER

Sometimes
I go about pitying myself
While I am carried by
The wind
Across the sky.

CHIPPEWA SONG

It was the wind that gave them life.
It is the wind that comes out of our mouths now
that gives us life.
When this ceases to blow we die.
In the skin at the tips of our fingers
we see the trail of the wind;
it shows us the wind blew
when our ancestors were created.

NAVAJO CHANT

148

Cover my earth mother four times with many flowers.
Let the heavens be covered with the banked-up clouds.
Let the earth be covered with fog; cover the earth with rains.
Great waters, rains, cover the earth. Lightning cover the earth.
Let thunder be heard over the earth; let thunder be heard;
Let thunder be heard over the six regions of the earth.

ZUNI PRAYER

Let the reeds pander to the wayward wind,
I am the mountain range
That determines the course of the wind.

Let the seaweed flatter the inconstant tide,
I am the moon
That controls the tide's ebb and flow.

Let the magnet succumb to the unbending north and south,
I am the great earth:
Only I have directions.

HUANG GUOBIN

They who have the ocean as their eldest
flow out of the sea, purifying themselves, never resting.
Indra, the bull with the thunderbolt, opened a way for them;
let the waters, who are goddesses, help me here now.

The waters of the sky or those that flow,
those that are dug out or those that arise by themselves,
those pure and clear waters that seek the ocean as their goal—
let the waters, who are goddesses, help me here and now.

Those in whose midst King Varuna moves,
looking down upon the truth and falsehood of people,
those pure and clear waters that drip honey—
let the waters, who are goddesses, help me here and now.

Those among whom King Varuna, and Soma, and all gods
drink in ecstasy the exhilarating nourishment,
those into whom Agni Of-all-men entered—
let the waters, who are goddesses, help me here and now.

HINDU PRAYER

We overcome this wind.
We desire the rain to fall,
     that it be poured in showers quickly.
Ah, thou rain, I adjure thee fall.
     If thou rainest, it is well.
A drizzling confusion.
If it rains and our food ripens, it is well.
If the young men sing, it is well.
A drizzling confusion.
If our grain ripens, it is well.
If our women rejoice,
If the children rejoice,
If the young men sing,
If the aged rejoice,
An overflowing in the granary,
A torrent in flow,
If the wind veers to the south, it is well.
If the rain veers to the south, it is well.

JOHN S. MBITI

White floating clouds,
Clouds like the plains,
Come and water the earth.
Sun embrace the earth
that she may be fruitful.
Moon, lion of the north,
Bear of the west,
Badger of the south,
Wolf of the east,
Eagle of the heavens,
Shrew of the earth,
Elder war hero,
Intercede with the cloud people for us
That they may water the earth.

SIA INDIAN PRAYER

Waters, you are the ones who bring us the life force.

Help us to find nourishment so that we may look upon great joy.

Let us share in the most delicious sap that you have, as if you were loving mothers.

Let us go straight to the house of the one for whom your waters give us life and give us birth.

For our well-being let the goddesses be an aid to us, the waters be for us to drink. Let them cause well-being and health to flow over us.

Mistresses of all the things that are chosen, rulers over all peoples, the waters are the ones I beg for a cure.

Soma has told me that within the waters are all cures and Agni who is salutary to all.

Waters, yield your cure as an armour for my body, so that I may see the sun for a long time.

Waters, carry far away all of this that has gone bad in me, either what I have done in malicious deceit or whatever lie I have sworn to.

I have sought the waters today; we have joined with their sap. O Agni full of moisture, come and flood me with splendour.

HINDU PRAYER

153

Water flows from high in the mountains.
    Water runs deep in the Earth.
Miraculously, water comes to us,
    and sustains all life.

THICH NHAT HANH

Water flows over these hands.
May I use them skillfully
to preserve our precious planet.

THICH NHAT HANH

What would the world be, once bereft
Of wet and of wildness? Let them be left,
O let them be left, wildness and wet;
Long live the weeds and the wilderness yet.

GERARD MANLEY HOPKINS

154

Do not stifle me with the strange scent
Of low growing mountain lilies—
Do not confuse me
With the salubrious odor of honeysuckle!

I cannot separate in my mind
Sweetness from sweetness—
Mimosa from wild white violets;
Magnolia from Cape Jasmine!

I am from the north tide country,
I can understand only the scent of seaweed;
Salt marsh and scrub pine
Riding on the breath of an amorous fog!

O do not confuse me
With sweetness upon sweetness;
Let me escape safely from this gentle madness—
Let me go back to the salt of sanity
In the scent of the sea . . . !

DONALD JEFFREY HAYES

Ice mountain melted
ages ago
    and made this ridge,
this place of changes.

Now we are rooted in it,
    we of the old ones,
    we of the new ones from afar;
oatgrass meadow, douglas fir thicket,
    we are rooted in the ridge of changes in the time of
        changes.

The winds carry strange smells; this is a day of change.

Great ones above and below, bless us!

O shining One above, feed us with your light!
O soft ones, sky darkeners, wash us with your raindrops!
O powers above us, bless us with your gifts,
    for we reach up to you,
    branching wood and sap.

O Earthmother from whom we grow,
    sandy gravel into whom our roots branch wood
        and sap deep down,
    bless us in our night-sleep, in our death and decay.

Bless us, dark earth as we give back
    that which we have received
    as we make a forest of blessing a ridge of blessing
    for the future to grow upon.

              CHINOOK PSALTER

Hail Mother, who art the earth,
Hallowed be thy soil, rocks and flora
    that nourish and support all life.
Blessed be thy wind that gives us breath
    and thy waters that quench, bathe and refresh
    all living things.
Holy Earth—as one—we praise your majesty,
    grace and wonder.

              BILL FAHERTY

Thank you Father for your free gift of fire.
Because it is through fire that you draw near to us every day.
It is with fire that you constantly bless us.
Our Father, bless this fire today.
With your power enter into it.
Make this fire a worthy thing.
A thing that carries your blessing.
Let it become a reminder of your love.
A reminder of life without end.
Make the life of these people to be baptised like this fire.
A thing that shines for the sake of people.
A thing that shines for your sake.
Father, heed this sweet smelling smoke.
Make their life also sweet smelling.
A thing sweet smelling that rises to God.
A holy thing.
A thing fitting for you.

MASAI PRAYER

Now this day, my Sun Father,
Now that you have come out standing
To your sacred place.

That from which we draw the water of life
Prayer meal—
Here I give unto you.

Your long life,
Your old age,
Your waters,
Your seeds,
Your riches,
Your power,
Your strong spirit.
Of all these, to me may you grant.

EGYPTIAN PRAYER TO SUN GOD

Wild air, world-mothering air,
Nestling me everywhere,
That each eyelash or hair
Girdles; goes home betwixt
The fleeciest, frailest-flixed
Snowflake; that's fairly mixed
With riddles, and is rife
In every least thing's life;
This needful, never spent,
And nursing element;
My more than meat and drink,
My meal at every wink;
This air, which, by life's law,
My lung must draw and draw
Now but to breathe its praise. . . .

GERARD MANLEY HOPKINS

Beseeching the breath of the divine one,
His life-giving breath,
His breath of old age,
His breath of waters,
His breath of seeds,
His breath of riches,
His breath of fecundity,
His breath of power
His breath of all good fortune,
Asking for his breath
And into my warm body drawing his breath,
I add to your breath
That happily you may always live.

ZUNI CHANT

Bakerwoman God,
I am your living bread,
Strong, brown Bakerwoman God.
I am your low, soft, and being-shaped loaf.
I am your rising
bread, well-kneaded
by some divine and knotty
pair of knuckles,
by your warm earth hands.
I am bread well-kneaded.

Put me in fire, Bakerwoman God,
put me in your own bright fire.

I am warm, warm as you from fire.
I am white and gold, soft and hard,
brown and round.
I am so warm from fire.

Break me, Bakerwoman God.
I am broken under your caring Word.
Drop me in your special juice in pieces.
Drop me in your blood.
Drunken me in the great red flood.
Self-giving chalice swallow me.
My skin shines in the divine wine.
My face is cup-covered and I drown.

I fall up
in a red pool
in a gold world
where your warm
sunskin hand is there
to catch and hold me.
Bakerwoman God, remake.

ALLA RENEE BOZARTH

O Lord,
One tiny bit of water rests on the palm of my hand.
I bring it to you and with it I bring the whole ocean.
This tiny drop has the power to ease the burning thirst of men;
when spread on the earth, to give life to the seed and the future
        harvest;
when poured on the fire to quench the blaze.
A tiny drop of water
can cleanse the whole of my impurity when blessed by your
forgiveness.

But, O Lord,
more than all this, this tiny drop of water passed over my head
is the symbol of my birth in You.

ISHPRIYA R.S.C.J.

164

What a thing it is to sit absolutely alone,
in the forest, at night, cherished by this
wonderful, unintelligible,
perfectly innocent speech,
the most comforting speech in the world,
the talk that rain makes by itself all over the ridges,
and the talk of the watercourses everywhere in the hollows!
Nobody started it, nobody is going to stop it.
It will talk as long as it wants, this rain.
As long as it talks I am going to listen.

THOMAS MERTON

I lie alone
remembering changes
how sudden crystals grew
from water falling
in a cup in a rock
surprising forms
acids in a cup in a rock
receiving lightning
a cup in a rock receiving
    lightning
I am here
I lie alone
no one completes me
after lightning
I bide my time
I hold my forms beyond
    surprising islands

I lie alone
remembering changes
how grinding ice came down
the slide of earth
rub of rivers
knuckles of trees cracking rocks
receiving ice surprising
cracking rocks receiving ice
a tree of rivers sprang inside
    me
I am here
I lie alone
no one completes me
after water
I bide my time
I hold my face beyond
    surprising rains

W. E. R. LA FARGE

Standing up on lifted, folded rock
looking out and down—

The creek falls to a far valley.
hills beyond that
facing, half-forested, dry
—clear sky
strong wind in the
stiff glittering needle clusters
of the pine—their brown
round trunk bodies
straight, still;
rustling trembling limbs and twigs

listen.

This living flowing land
is all there is, forever

We are it
it sings through us—

We could live on this Earth
without clothes or tools!

GARY SNYDER

VI

BLESSINGS AND
INVOCATIONS

More things are wrought by prayer
than this world dreams of.[1]

Every prayer carries a quality of engagement within it. It is a means of acting upon ourselves; of bringing ourselves into alignment with the rest of creation. Prayers of invocation and blessing seem particularly suited to this purpose. They directly express our intention and are uttered in order that some effect may be achieved. Our ability to offer an invocation or a blessing is equated with inner wisdom and power, for through their words and in their resonance we become mindful co-creators in this unfolding universe.

> *This is what I want to happen: that our earth mother*
> *may be clothed in ground corn four times over . . .*
> *In order that the country may be this way*
> *I have made my prayer sticks into something alive.*[2]

There is a sense of magic to some of the prayers in this section. Not the superstitious sort we usually think of, but rather in the ecological sense of the malleability—the creative flux—of all things. Things are not perceived as inert but as viable and alive, and since all that is alive necessarily grows and changes, then all existence can be affected under certain conditions and according to certain patterns. Through our blessings and invocations we acknowledge this network of forces that flows through the world, awakening the deeper levels of our consciousness to effect these patterns of change.

Implicit in these prayers is the principle that the part contains the whole. In a classic Buddhist sutra there is an extraordinary description of this holographic view of reality: The heaven of Indra is said to be a network of pearls so arranged that if you look at one you see all the others reflected in it. In the same way some scientists now recognize that each object in the world is not merely itself but involves every other object. All events are in some way interdependent, and everything we do affects the whole.

Invoking the powers of the universe or bestowing our blessing on the Earth or other beings is neither a simple benevolent wish nor an act of hubris. Rather it is an act of creative confidence. Emptied of the needs of our personality, our ego, or the demands of our society, we free ourselves to come into dynamic relationship with the whole universe. "May all beings be happy!"

---

[1]Alfred Lord Tennyson
[2]Zuni prayer

Deep peace of the running wave to you,
of water flowing, rising and falling,
sometimes advancing, sometimes receding . . .
May the stream of your life flow unimpeded!
Deep peace of the running wave to you!

Deep peace of the flowing air to you,
which fans your face on a sultry day,
the air which you breathe deeply, rhythmically,
which imparts to you energy, consciousness, life.
Deep peace of the flowing air to you!

Deep peace of the quiet earth to you,
who, herself unmoving, harbours the movements
and facilitates the life of the ten thousand creatures,
while resting contented, stable, tranquil.
Deep peace of the quiet earth to you!

Deep peace of the shining stars to you,
which stay invisible till darkness falls
and discloses their pure and shining presence
beaming down in compassion on our turning world.
Deep peace of the shining stars to you!

Deep peace of the watching shepherds to you,
of unpretentious folk who, watching and waiting,
spend long hours out on the hillside,

expecting in simplicity some Coming of the Lord.
Deep peace of the watching shepherds to you!

Deep peace of the Son of Peace to you,
who, swift as the wave and pervasive as the air,
quiet as the earth and shining like a star,
breathes into us His Peace and His Spirit.
Deep peace of the Son of Peace to you!

MARY ROGERS, ADAPTED FROM THE GAELIC

Peace be to earth and to airy space!
Peace be to heaven, peace to the waters,
Peace to the plant and peace to the trees!
May all the powers grant to me peace!
By this invocation of peace may peace be diffused!
By this invocation of peace may peace bring peace!
With this peace the dreadful I now appease,
With this peace the cruel I now appease,
With this peace all evil I now appease,
So that peace may prevail, happiness prevail!
May everything for us be peaceful!

ATHARVA VEDA XIX

173

My brother the star, my mother the earth,
My father the sun, my sister the moon
to my life give beauty, to my body give strength,
to my work give goodness, to my house give peace
to my spirit give truth, to my elders give wisdom.

We must pray for strength.
We must pray to come together,
Pray to the weeping earth,
pray to the trembling waters
and to the wandering rain.
We must pray to the whispering moon,
pray to the tip-toeing stars
and to the hollering sun.

NANCY WOOD

May the wind blow sweetness,
the rivers flow sweetness,
the herbs grow sweetness,
for the People of Truth!

Sweet be the night,
sweet the dawn,
sweet be earth's fragrance,
sweet be our Heaven!

May the tree afford us sweetness,
the sun shine sweetness,
our cows yield sweetness—
milk in plenty!

RIG VEDA I

Earth teach me stillness
    as the grasses are stilled with light.
Earth teach me suffering
    as old stones suffer with memory.
Earth teach me humility
    as blossoms are humble with beginning.
Earth teach me caring
    as the mother who secures her young.
Earth teach me courage
    as the tree which stands all alone.
Earth teach me limitation
    as the ant which crawls on the ground.
Earth teach me freedom
    as the eagle which soars in the sky.
Earth teach me resignation
    as the leaves which die in the fall.
Earth teach me regeneration
    as the seed which rises in the spring.
Earth teach me to forget myself
    as melted snow forgets its life.
Earth teach me to remember kindness
    as dry fields weep with rain.

UTE PRAYER

Spirit of God in the clear running water,
blowing to greatness the trees on the hill,
Spirit of God in the finger of morning,
fill the earth, bring it to birth and blow where You
        will.
Blow, blow, blow till I be but breath of the Spirit
        blowing in me.

Down in the meadows the willows are moaning,
sheep in the pasture land cannot lie still.
Spirit of God, creation is groaning
fill the earth, bring it to birth and blow where You
        will.
Blow, blow, blow till I be but breath of the Spirit
        blowing in me.

Spirit of God, every man's heart is lonely
watching and waiting and hungry until,
Spirit of God, man longs that you only
fulfill the earth, bring it to birth and blow where
        You will.
Blow, blow, blow till I be but breath of the Spirit
        blowing in me.

EAST AFRICAN MEDICAL MISSIONARY SISTERS

This is what I want to happen: that our earth mother
may be clothed in ground corn four times over;
that frost flowers cover her over entirely;
that the mountain pines far away over there
may stand close to each other in the cold;
that the weight of snow crack some branches!
In order that the country may be this way
I have made my prayer sticks into something alive.

ZUNI PRAYER

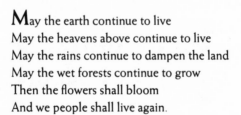

May the earth continue to live
May the heavens above continue to live
May the rains continue to dampen the land
May the wet forests continue to grow
Then the flowers shall bloom
And we people shall live again.

HAWAIIAN PRAYER

Mother, Father, God, Universal Power.
Remind us daily of the sanctity of all life.

Touch our hearts with the glorious oneness
of all creation,
As we strive to respect all the living beings
on this planet.

Penetrate our souls with the beauty of this
earth,
As we attune ourselves to the rhythm and
flow of the seasons.

Awaken our minds with the knowledge to
achieve a world in perfect harmony
And grant us the wisdom to realize that we
can have heaven on earth.

JO POORE

May all I say and all I think
    be in harmony with thee,
God within me, God beyond me,
    maker of the trees.

In me be the windswept truth of shorepine,
    fragrance of balsam and spruce,
        the grace of hemlock.
In me the truth of douglas fir, straight, tall,
    strong-trunked land hero of fireproof bark.
Sheltering tree of life, cedar's truth be mine,
    cypress truth, juniper aroma, strength of yew.

May all I say and all I think
    be in harmony with thee,
God within me, God beyond me,
    maker of the trees.

In me be the truth of streamlover willow
    soil-giving alder
    hazel of sweet nuts, wisdom-branching oak.
In me the joy of crabapple, greatmaple, vinemaple,
    cleansing cascara and lovely dogwood.
And the gracious truth of the copper branched arbutus,
    bright with colour and fragrance,
        be with me on the Earth.

May all I say and all I think
be in harmony with thee,
God within me, God beyond me,
maker of the trees.

CHINOOK PSALTER

I who am the beauty of the green earth and the white moon among the stars and the mysteries of the waters, I call upon your soul to arise and come unto Me. For I am the soul of nature that gives life to the universe. From Me all things proceed and unto Me they must return. Let My worship be in the heart that rejoices, for behold—all acts of love and pleasure are My rituals. Let there be beauty and strength, power and compassion, honor and humility, mirth and reverence within you. And you who seek to know Me, know that your seeking and yearning will avail you not, unless you know the Mystery: for if that which you seek, you find not within yourself, you will never find it without. For behold, I have been with you from the beginning, and I am that which is attained at the end of desire.

DOREEN VALIENTE

Only the winds of spring
can open the anemone
wrote Pliny

Windflower
mayflower
nimbleweed
Anemone quinquefolia
the wind-god's
name in spring

Five white petals
three-part leaves—
the ancients picked them
chanting prayers

Help us
   to protect these waters
these wild lands you open on
instill in us
   the powers
   to contain the ooze of mines
the excrement of need

Protect these
aquifers and springs
   of highland rock
the breath of winds
we blossom by

WALT FRANKLIN

Sensuous during life
   do not deny me in death!

Wash me with scent of apple blossom.

Anoint me with essence of lilac.

Fill my veins with honeysuckle nectar.

Sprinkle me with perfume of purple violets.

Envelop me in shroud saturated with fragrance of freshly
   mown meadow hay.

Rest me in moss velvet earth.

Cover me with soil exuding flavor of maple and oak leaves.

Command a white birch to stand guard!

LOIS WICKENHAUSER

Grandfather Great Spirit
All over the world the faces of living ones
        are alike.
With tenderness they have come up out
        of the ground.
Look upon your children that they may
face the winds and walk the good road to
        the Day of Quiet.
Grandfather Great Spirit
Fill us with the Light.
Give us the strength to understand,
and the eyes to see.
Teach us to walk the soft Earth as relatives
        to all that live.

SIOUX PRAYER

Soul of Earth, sanctify me.
Body of Earth, save me.
Blood of Earth, fill me with love.
Water from Earth's side, wash me.
Passion of Earth, strengthen me.
Resurrection of Earth, empower me.
Good Earth, hear me.
Within your wounds, hide me.
Never let me be separated from you.
From the power of evil, protect me.
At the hour of my death, call me
That with your living ones I may thank you
For all eternity. Amen.

ADAPTED BY JANE PELLOWSKI
FROM *ANIMA CHRISTI*

Kali, be with us.
Violence, destruction, receive our homage.
Help us to bring darkness into the light,
To lift out the pain, the anger,
Where it can be seen for what it is—
The balance-wheel for our vulnerable, aching love.
Within the act of creation,
Crude power that forges a balance
Between hate and love.

Help us to be the always hopeful
Gardeners of the spirit
Who know that without darkness
Nothing comes to birth
As without light
Nothing flowers.

Bear the roots in mind,
You, the dark one, Kali,
Awesome power.

MAY SARTON

To all that is brief and fragile
superficial, unstable,
To all that lacks foundation
argument or principles;
To all that is light,
fleeting, changing, finite
To smoke spirals,
wand roses,
To sea foam
and mists of oblivion. . . .
To all that is light in weight
for itinerants
on this transient earth
Somber, raving,
with transitory words
and vaporous bubbly wines
I toast
in breakable glasses. . . .

MARIA EUGENIA BAZ FERREIRA

O Great Spirit
Whose voice I hear in the winds,
and whose breath gives life to all the world,
hear me! I am small and weak, I need your strength
     and wisdom.

Let me walk in beauty, and make my eyes
     ever behold the red and purple sunset.

Make my hands respect the things you have made
     and my ears sharp to hear your voice.

Make me wise so that I may understand the things
     you have taught my people.

Let me learn the lessons you have hidden in every
     leaf and rock.

I seek strength, not to be greater than my brother,
     but to fight my greatest enemy—myself.

Make me always ready to come to you with clean
     hands and straight eyes.

So when life fades, as the fading sunset,
my spirit may come to you without shame.

TRADITIONAL NATIVE AMERICAN PRAYER

188

O our Father, the Sky, hear us
   and make us strong.
O our Mother the Earth, hear us
   and give us support.
O Spirit of the East,
   send us your Wisdom.
O Spirit of the South,
   may we tread your path of life.
O Spirit of the West,
   may we always be ready for the long journey.
O Spirit of the North, purify us
   with your cleansing winds.

SIOUX PRAYER

At Tara today in this fateful hour
I place all heaven with its power,
And the sun with its brightness,
And the snow with its whiteness,
And fire with all the strength it has,
And lightning with its rapid wrath,
And the winds with their swiftness along the path,
And the sea with its deepness,
And the rocks with their steepness
And the Earth with its starkness;
All these I place
By God's almighty help and grace,
Between myself and the powers of Darkness.

I arise today
Through a mighty strength, the invocation of the Trinity,
Through belief in the threeness,
Through confession of the oneness
Of the Creator of Creation.

I arise today
Through the strength of heaven;
Light of sun,
Radiance of moon,
Splendor of fire,
Speed of lightning,
Swiftness of wind,
Depth of sea,
Stability of earth,
Firmness of rock.

I arise today,
Through a mighty strength, the invocation of the Trinity,
Through belief in the threeness,
Through confession of the oneness
Of the Creator of Creation.

SAINT PATRICK

Oh Great Spirit of the North,
we come to you and ask for the
strength and the power
to bear what is cold and harsh in life.
We come like the buffalo
ready to receive the winds that
truly can be overwhelming at times.
Whatever is cold and uncertain in our life,
we ask you to give us the strength to bear it.
Do not let the winter blow us away.
Oh Spirit of Life and Spirit of the North,
we ask you for strength and for warmth.

Oh Great Spirit of the East,
we turn to you where the sun comes up,
from where the power of light and refreshment come.
Everything that is born comes up in this direction—
the birth of babies, the birth of the puppies,
the birth of ideas and the birth of friendship.
Let there be the light.
Oh Spirit of the East,
let the color of fresh rising in our life
be glory to you.

Oh Great Spirit of the South,
spirit of all that is warm and gentle and refreshing,
we ask you to give us this spirit
of growth, of fertility, of gentleness.
Caress us with a cool breeze when the days are hot.
Give us seeds that the flowers, trees and fruits
of the earth may grow.
Give us the warmth of good friendships.
Oh Spirit of the South,
send the warmth and the growth of your blessings.

Oh Great Spirit of the West,
where the sun goes down each day to come up the next,
we turn to you in praise of sunsets
and in thanksgiving for changes.
You are the great colored sunset of the red west
which illuminates us.
You are the powerful cycle which pulls us to transformation.
We ask for the blessings of the sunset.
Keep us open to life's changes.
Oh Spirit of the West,
when it is time for us to go into the earth,
do not desert us, but receive us in the arms of our loved ones.

DIANN NEU

From the East House of Light
May wisdom dawn in us
So we may see all things in clarity

From the North House of Night
May wisdom ripen in us
So we may know all from within

From the West House of Transformation
May wisdom be transformed into right
    action
So we may do what must be done

From the South House of the Eternal Sun
May right action reap the harvest
So we may enjoy the fruits of planetary being

From Above House of Heaven
Where star people and ancestors gather
May their blessings come to us now

From Below House of Earth
May the heartbeat of her crystal core
Bless us with harmonies to end all war

From the Center Galactic Source
Which is everywhere at once
May everything be known as the light of mutual love

OH YUM HUNAB K'U
EVAM MAYA E MA HO!

JOSÉ ARGUËLLES

O Hidden Life vibrant in every atom;
O Hidden Light! shining in every creature;
O Hidden Love! embracing all in Oneness;
May each who feels himself as one with Thee,
Know he is also one with every other.

ANNIE BESANT

Remember, remember the circle of the sky
the stars and the brown eagle
the supernatural winds
breathing night and day
from the four directions

Remember, remember the great life of the sun
breathing on the earth
it lies upon the earth
to bring out life upon the earth
life covering the earth

Remember, remember the sacredness of things
running streams and dwellings
the young within the nest
a hearth for sacred fire
the holy flame of fire

PAWNEE/OSAGE/OMAHA INDIAN SONG

O Lady
the hem of whose garment
is the sky, whose grace
falls from her glance, who gives
life from the touch of one finger
O Lady
whose hair is the willow, whose breath
is the riversong, who lopes
thru the milky way, baying, stars
going out, O
Lady whose deathshead holds a thousand eyes
eye sockets black imploded stars, who trails
frail as a northern virgin on the mist, O
Lady fling your bright drops to us, emblems
of your love, throw
your green scarf on the battered earth once more
O smile, disrobe for us, unveil
your eyes

DIANE DI PRIMA

Blessing of galaxies, blessing of stars:
>   Great stars, small stars, red stars, blue ones.
Blessing of nebula, blessing of supernova,
>   Planets, satellites, asteroids, comets.

Blessing of our sun and moon, blessing of our earth;
>   Oceans, rivers, continents, mountain ranges
Blessing of wind and cloud, blessing of rain;
>   Fog bank, snowdrift, lightning and thunder.

Bless the wisdom of the holy one above us.
Bless the truth of the holy one beneath us.
Bless the love of the holy one within us.

Blessing of green plants, blessing of forests:
    Cedar, douglas fir, swordfern, salal bush
Blessing of fish and birds, blessing of mammals:
    Salmon, eagle, cougar and mountain goat.

May all humankind likewise offer blessing:
    Old woman, young woman, wise men and foolish
Blessing of youthfulness, blessing of children
    Big boys, little boys, big girls and little ones.

Bless the wisdom of the holy one above us;
Bless the truth of the holy one beneath us;
Bless the love of the holy one within us.

CHINOOK PSALTER

Blessed be you, harsh matter, barren soil, stubborn rock:
you who yield only to force, you who cause us to work
if we would eat.

Blessed be you, perilous matter, violent sea, untamable passion:
you who, unless we fetter you, will devour us.

Blessed be you, mighty matter, irresistible march of evolution,
reality ever new-born; you who, by constantly shattering
our mental categories, force us to go ever further and further
in our pursuit of the truth.

Blessed be you, universal matter, immeasurable time,
boundless ether, triple abyss of stars and atoms and generations:
you who by overflowing and dissolving our narrow standards
or measurements reveal to us the dimensions of God.

Blessed be you, impenetrable matter: you who, interposed
between our minds and the world of essences, cause us to languish
with the desire to pierce through the seamless veil of phenomena.

Blessed be you, mortal matter: you who one day will undergo
the process of dissolution within us and will thereby take us
forcibly into the very heart of that which exists.

You who batter us and then dress our wounds,
you who resist and yield to us,
you who wreck and build,
you who shackle and liberate,
the sap of our souls,
the hand of God,
the flesh of Christ:
it is you, matter, that I bless.

PIERRE TEILHARD DE CHARDIN

O God,
creator of our land,
our earth, the trees,
the animals and humans,
all is for your honour.

The drums beat it out,
and people sing about it,
and they dance with noisy joy
that you are the Lord.

You also have pulled the other continents
out of the sea.
What a wonderful world you have made
out of wet mud,
and what beautiful men and women!
We thank you for all the beauty of this earth.

The grace of your creation is like a cool day
between rainy seasons.
We drink in your creation with our eyes.
We listen to the birds' jubilee
with our ears.

How strong and good
and sure your earth smells,
and everything that grows there.

Bless us.
Bless our land and people.
Bless our forests with mahogany,
wawa, and cacao.
Bless our fields with cassava and peanuts.
Bless the waters
that flow through our land.

Fill them with fish
and drive great schools of fish to our seacoast,
so that the fishermen in their unsteady boats
do not need to go out too far.

Be with us in our countries
and in all Africa,
and in the whole world.
Prepare us for the service that we should render.

ASHANTI PRAYER

May the blessing of light be on you, light without and light within. May the blessed sunshine shine on you and warm your heart till it glows like a great peat fire, so that the stranger may come and warm himself at it, and also a friend.

And may the light shine out of the two eyes of you, like a candle set in the two windows of a house, bidding the wanderer come in out of the storm; and may the blessings of the rain be on you—the soft, sweet rain. May it fall upon your spirit so that all the little flowers may spring up and shed their sweetness on the air. And may the blessings of the Great Rains be on you, may they beat upon your spirit and wash it fair and clean, and leave there many a shining pool where the blue of heaven shines, and sometimes a star.

And may the blessing of the Earth be on you—the great round earth; may you ever have a kindly greeting for those you pass as you're going along the roads. May the earth be soft under you when you rest upon it, tired at the end of a day, and may it rest easy over you when at the last, you lay out under it; may it rest so lightly over you that your soul may be off from under it quickly and up and off, and on its way to God. And now may the Lord bless you all and bless you kindly.

TRADITIONAL IRISH BLESSING

Blessed be the works of your hands,
  O Holy One.
Blessed be these hands that have touched life.
Blessed be these hands that have nurtured creativity.
Blessed be these hands that have held pain.
Blessed be these hands that have embraced with passion.
Blessed be these hands that have tended gardens.
Blessed be these hands that have closed in anger.
Blessed be these hands that have planted new seeds.
Blessed be these hands that have harvested ripe fields.
Blessed be these hands that have cleaned, washed,
    mopped, scrubbed.
Blessed be these hands that have become knotty with age.
Blessed be these hands that are wrinkled and scarred
    from doing justice.
Blessed be these hands that have reached out and been
    received.
Blessed be these hands that hold the promise of the
    future.
Blessed be the works of your hands,
  O Holy One.

DIANN NEU

Not with my hands
But with my heart I bless you:
May peace forever dwell
Within your breast!

May Truth's white light
Move with you and possess you—
And may your thoughts and words
Wear her bright crest!

May Time move down
Its endless path of beauty
Conscious of you
And better for your being!

Spring after Spring
Array itself in splendor
Seeking the favor
Of your sentient seeing!

May hills lean toward you,
Hills and windswept mountains,
And trees be happy
That have seen you pass—

Your eyes dark kinsmen
To the stars above you—
Your feet remembered
By the blades of grass . . . !

DONALD JEFFREY HAYES

O bless this people, Lord, who seek their own face
Under the mask and can hardly recognize it . . .

O bless this people that breaks its bond . . .

And with them, all the peoples of Europe,
All the peoples of Asia,
All the peoples of Africa,
All the peoples of America,
Who sweat blood and sufferings.

And see, in the midst of these millions of waves
The sea swell of the heads of my people.
And grant to their warm hands that they may clasp
The earth in a girdle of brotherly hands,
Beneath the rainbow of thy peace.

LEOPOLD SEDAR SENGHOR

Benedicto: May your trails be crooked, winding, lonesome,
dangerous, leading to the most amazing view.
May your rivers flow without end,
meandering through pastoral valleys tinkling with bells,
past temples and castles and poets' towers
into a dark primeval forest where tigers belch and monkeys howl,
through miasmal and mysterious swamps and down into a desert
    of red rock,
blue mesas, domes and pinnacles and grottos of endless stone,
and down again into a deep vast ancient unknown chasm
where bars of sunlight blaze on profiled cliffs,
where deer walk across the white sand beaches,
where storms come and go
as lightning clangs upon the high crags,
where something strange and more beautiful
and more full of wonder than your deepest dreams
waits for you—
beyond that next turning of the canyon walls.

EDWARD ABBEY

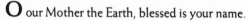

O our Mother the Earth, blessed is your name.

Blessed are your fields and forests, your rocks and mountains, your grasses and trees and flowers, and every green and growing thing.

Blessed are your streams and lakes and rivers, the oceans where our life began, and all your waters that sustain our bodies and refresh our souls.

Blessed is the air we breathe, your atmosphere, that surrounds us and binds us to every living thing.

Blessed are all creatures who walk along your surface or swim in your waters or fly through your air, for they are all our relatives.

Blessed are all people who share this planet, for we are all one family, and the same spirit moves through us all.

Blessed is the sun, our day star, bringer of morning and the heat of summer, giver of light and life.

Blessed is the moon, our night lamp, ruler of the tides, protector of all women, and guardian of our dreams.

Blessed are the stars and planets, the time-keepers, who fill our nights with beauty and our hearts with awe.

O Great Spirit whose voice we hear in the wind and whose face we see in the morning sun, blessed is your name.

Help us to remember that you are everywhere, and teach us the way of peace.

HELEN WEAVER

VII

PRAISE AND
THANKSGIVING

AT THE HEART OF EARTH

Prayer is a sense of belonging. Belonging is the basic truth of our existence. We belong here. Life belongs here. Likewise, at the heart of gratefulness, in its deepest sense, we also find an expression of belonging. When we say "Thank you" we really are saying "We belong together." That is why we sometimes find it so difficult to say "Thank you"—because we don't want to acknowledge our interdependence. We don't want to be obliged. But in a healthy society that is exactly what we seek: mutual obligations. Everyone is obliged to everyone and everything else; we all belong together, we are *of* each other. In this awareness we are freed from self-preoccupation—and only then, emptied of self, can we be filled with thanks. As Brother David Steindl-Rast tells us, "Love whole-heartedly, be surprised, give thanks and praise—then you will discover the fullness of your life."

Within this human impulse to gratitude flow the vast cycles of universal reciprocity—for everything that is taken, something has to be given in return. If you merely take in a breath and stop there, you will die. Likewise if you merely breathe out. Life is not giving or taking, but give *and* take. This is the dynamic expression of universal belonging expressed in our thanksgiving.

> *We give-away our thanks to the earth*
> *   which gives us our home.*
> *We give-away our thanks to the rivers and lakes*
> *   which give-away their water.*
> *We give-away our thanks to the trees*
> *   which give-away fruit and nuts. . . .*
>
> *All beings on earth: the trees, the animals, the wind*
> *   and the rivers give-away to one another*
> *   so all is in balance. . . .*[1]

In the midst of a pragmatic world in which we constantly ask ourselves how "useful" things are, these prayers may seem "useless." Yet perhaps the greatest gift we humans have to offer the rest of creation is our heartfelt appreciation. The ability to receive in thankfulness the blessings of life is an awesome quality. We alone on this planet can reflect on all that surrounds us and through our loving recognition the rest of the Earth achieves a deep fulfillment.

> *Earth isn't this what you want: invisibly*
> *to arise in us?*[2]

Our praise and thanksgiving is as essential a part of life's give and take as are the cycles of oxygen and water or any other nourishment flowing through the biosphere. For millennia prayers and songs like the ones in this chapter have been offered up to celebrate the miracle of existence of which we are part. May their voices join our own.

[1]Dolores La Chapelle
[2]Rainer Maria Rilke

I will sing of the well-founded Earth,
Mother of all, eldest of all beings.
She feeds all creatures that are in the world,
all that go upon the goodly land,
all that are in the paths of the seas,
and all that fly;
all these are fed of her store.

Through you, O Queen, we are blessed
in our children, and in our harvest
and to you we owe our lives.

Happy are we, who you delight to honour!
We have all things abundantly:
our houses are filled with good things,
our cities are orderly,
our sons exult with everfresh delight
and our daughters with flower laden hands
play and skip merrily over the soft flowers of the field.
Thus it is for those whom you honour,
O holy Goddess, Bountiful spirit!

Hail Earth, mother of the gods,
freely bestow upon me for this my song
that cheers the heart!

HOMERIS HYMNS XXX, ADAPTED BY ELIZABETH ROBERTS

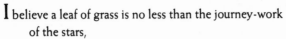

I believe a leaf of grass is no less than the journey-work
     of the stars,
And the pismire is equally perfect, and a grain of sand, and
     the egg of the wren,
And the tree-toad is a chef-d'oeuvre for the highest,
And the running blackberry would adorn the parlors of
     heaven,
And the narrowest hinge in my hand puts to scorn all machinery,
And the cow crunching with depress'd head surpasses any
     statue,
And a mouse is miracle enough to stagger sextillions of infidels.

WALT WHITMAN

Praise the Lord in your infinite variety all creatures,
minute and enormous in your verity
whose particular and unique features
are the context of his glory and his fecundity
Praise the Lord nebulae like grains of dust
silhouetted and fixed on photographic plates
Sirius, that dog star and his confederates
Arcturus, Antares, Aldebaran, the red bull
God's cup brimming over and ever full
Praise the Lord you his meteorites and comets
In your elliptical orbits and made planets
Praise the Lord atoms and molecules
Protons and electrons and all the stars
the minute protozoa, in their liquid, the radiolaria
Praise the Lord cetaceans and atomic submarines
for you are of God's mind in your particulars
Birds, the eagle and wren, the aeroplanes
and prisms in emerald copper sulphate

in the electronic microscope infinite
Coloured flowers blooming at the bottom of the sea,
diatoms and the diadems of the Antilles
Like a rose of diamonds, let all these
and the unended maritime fauna
praise the Lord, and the Tropic of Cancer
storms of the North Atlantic and the Humboldt current,
the dark, sweating forests of the Amazon
the shining island jewels of the South Ocean
volcanoes and lagoons and the Caribbean
behind the silhouettes of the infinite palm
democratic republics, the United Nations
praise the Lord as even for police is appropriate
the students, the young, the beautiful,
His glory surpasses the heavens, it is bountiful
telescope and microscope seeing near and far
It is he who has made the people plentiful
Who would not yield to the Lord the word hosanna?

ERNESTO CARDENAL

Glory be to God for dappled things—
      For skies of couple-colour as a brinded cow;
            For rose-moles all in stipple upon trout that swim;
Fresh-firecoal chestnut falls; finches' wings;
      Landscape plotted and pieced—fold, fallow, and plough;
            And all trades, their gear and tackle and trim.
All things counter, original, spare, strange;
      Whatever is fickle, freckled (who knows how?)
            With swift, slow; sweet, sour; adazzle, dim;
He fathers-forth whose beauty is past change:
            Praise him.

GERARD MANLEY HOPKINS

All you big things, bless the Lord
Mount Kilimanjaro and Lake Victoria
The Rift Valley and the Serengeti Plain
Fat baobabs and shady mango trees
All eucalyptus and tamarind trees
Bless the Lord
Praise and extol Him for ever and ever.

All you tiny things, bless the Lord
Busy black ants and hopping fleas
Wriggling tadpoles and mosquito larvae
Flying locusts and water drops
Pollen dust and tsetse flies
Millet seeds and dried dagaa
Bless the Lord
Praise and extol Him for ever and ever.

AFRICAN CANTICLE

Praise the world to the angel, not the unutterable
      world;
you cannot astonish him with your glorious feelings;
in the universe, where he feels more sensitively,
you're just a beginner. Therefore, show him the simple
that lives near our hands and eyes as our very own.
Tell him about the Things. He'll stand more amazed,
      as you stood
beside the rope-maker in Rome, or the potter on the
      Nile
Show him how happy a thing can be, how blameless
      and ours;
how even the lamentation of sorrow purely decides
to take form, serves as a thing, or dies
in a thing, and blissfully in the beyond
escapes the violin. And these things that live,
slipping away, understand that you praise them;
transitory themselves, they trust us for rescue,
us, the most transient of all. They wish us to
      transmute them
in our invisible heart—oh, infinitely into us!
      Whoever we are.

Earth isn't this what you want: invisibly
to arise in us? Is it not your dream
to be some day invisible? Earth! Invisible!
What, if not transformation, is your insistent
        commission?
Earth, dear one, I will! Oh, believe it needs
not one more of your springtimes to win me over.
One, just one, is already too much for my blood.
From afar I'm utterly determined to be yours.
You were always right and your sacred revelation
        is the intimate death.
Behold, I'm alive. On what? Neither childhood nor
        future
grows less . . . surplus of existence
is welling up in my heart.

RAINER MARIA RILKE

Praise wet snow
        falling early.
Praise the shadow
        my neighbor's chimney casts on the tile roof
even this gray October day that should, they say,
have been golden.
                        Praise
the invisible sun burning beyond
        the white cold sky, giving us
light and the chimney's shadow.
Praise
god or the gods, the unknown,
that which imagined us, which stays
our hand,
our murderous hand,
                        and gives us
still,
in the shadow of death,
        our daily life,
        and the dream still
of goodwill, of peace on earth.
Praise
flow and change, night and
the pulse of day.

DENISE LEVERTOV

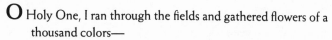

O Holy One, I ran through the fields and gathered flowers of a
thousand colors—
And now I pour them out at Your feet.
Their beauty and their brightness shout for joy in Your Presence.
You created the flowers of the fields and made each one far more
lovely
than all the skill of man could design.
Accept my joy along with theirs,
this field of blossoms at Your feet.
Holy One
as the wind blows through these flowers
till they dance in the ecstasy of creation,
send Your Spirit to blow through my being
till I too bloom and dance with the fulness of Your life.

ISHPRIYA R.S.C.J.

Bless the Lord, O my soul
Lord my God you are great
　　You are clothed with the energy of atoms
　　as with a mantle
From a cloud of whirling cosmic dust
as on the potter's wheel
you began to tease out the whorls of the galaxies
and the gas escapes from your fingers condensing and burning
and you were fashioning the stars
You made a spatterdash of planets like spores or seeds
and scattered comets like flowers. . . .

ERNESTO CARDENAL

Bless Thee, O Lord, for the living arc of the sky over me this morning.

Bless Thee, O Lord, for the companionship of night mist far above the skyscraper peaks I saw when I woke once during the night.

Bless Thee, O Lord, for the miracle of light to my eyes and the mystery of it ever changing.

Bless Thee, O Lord, for the laws Thou hast ordained holding fast these tall oblongs of stone and steel, holding fast the planet Earth in its course and farther beyond the cycle of the Sun.

CARL SANDBURG

Be praised my lord with all your creatures
but especially with Brother Sun
because you show us light and day through him
and he is lovely glowing with great shine
from you my lord: his definition

Be praised my lord for Brother Wind
and for the air and cloudy days
and bright and all days else because
through these you give your creatures
sustenance

Be praised my lord for Sister Water
because she shows great use and humbleness in hers and
        preciousness
and depth

Be praised my lord for Brother Fire
through whom you light all nights upon the earth
Because he too is lovely
full of joy and manly strength

Be praised my lord because our sister
Mother Earth sustains and rules
us and because she raises
food to feed us: colored flowers
grass

Be praised my lord for those who pardon by your love
and suffer illness and grief
Bless those who undergo in silence
the poor for whom you hold a crown

Be praised my lord for Sister Death-of-Body
whom no man living will escape
And pity those who die in mortal sin
and everyone she finds who minds you
bless: no second death
to bring them hurt

Oh praise my lord and bless my lord and thank
and serve my lord with humbleness
Triumphant

SAINT FRANCIS OF ASSISI

For the marvelous grace of Your Creation—
We pour out our thanks to You, our God,
    for sun and moon and stars,
    for rain and dew and winds,
    for winter cold and summer heat.

We pour forth our praise to You
    for mountains and hills,
    for springs and valleys,
    for rivers and seas.

We praise You, O Lord,
    for plants growing in earth and water,
    for life inhabiting lakes and seas,
    for life creeping in soils and land,
    for creatures living in wetlands and waters,
    for life flying above earth and sea,
    for beasts dwelling in woods and fields.

How many and wonderful are Your works, our God!
    In wisdom you have made them all!

But we confess, dear Lord,
    as creatures privileged with the care and keeping of Your
        Creation
    that we have abused your Creation gifts
    through arrogance, ignorance, and greed.

We confess risking permanent damage to Your handiwork;
    we confess impoverishing Creation's ability to bring You
        praise.

Yet, we confess that Your handiwork displays Your glory,
    leaving all of us without excuse
    but to know You
We confess that Your handiwork
    provides the context of our living;
    it is our home,
    it is the realm in which we live the life of Your kingdom:
    Your kingdom that is now in our midst and coming yet more
        fully.
We confess, Lord, that we often are unaware
    of how deeply we have hurt Your good earth
    and its marvelous gifts.
We confess that we often are unaware
    of how our abuse of Creation has also been an abuse of
        ourselves.

O Lord, how long will it take before we awaken to what we have
        done?
    How many waters must we pollute?
    How many woodlots must we destroy?
    How many forests must we despoil?
    How much soil must we erode and poison, O Lord?

229

How much of Earth's atmosphere must we contaminate?
>   How many species must we abuse and extinguish?
>   How many people must we degrade and kill with toxic
>   wastes
>   before we learn to love and respect your Creation;
>   before we learn to love and respect our home?

For our wrongs, Lord, we ask forgiveness.

In sorrow for what we have done
>   we offer our repentance.
We pray that our actions toward You and Your Creation
>   are worthy of our repentance;
>   that we will so act here on earth that heaven will not be a
>   shock to us.

We promise to reverence Your Creation as a gracious gift
>   entrusted to us by You, our God.
We promise anew to be stewards
>   and not pillagers
>   of what You have entrusted to us.

Creator God,
>   You have given us every reason
>   to learn and promote this wisdom of lives lived in harmony
>   with Creation.

May we, your servants, increasingly serve.

May we, your servants, increasingly come to love Your Creation
   as we increasingly come to love You,

through Christ Jesus,
our Lord.

Amen.

NORTH AMERICAN CONFERENCE
ON CHRISTIANITY AND ECOLOGY

231

O Lord, how lovely it is to be your guest.
Breeze full of scents; mountains reaching to the skies;
Waters like a boundless mirror,
Reflecting the sun's golden rays and the scudding clouds
All nature murmurs mysteriously, breathing depths of tenderness.
Birds and beasts of the forest bear the imprint of your love.
Blessed are you, mother earth, in your floating loveliness,
Which wakens our yearning for happiness that will last forever
In the land where, amid beauty that grows not old,
Rings out the cry: Alleluia!

What sort of praises can I give you?
I have never heard the song of the cherubim,
A joy reserved for the spirits above
But I know the praises that nature sings to you.
In winter, I have beheld how silently in the moonlight
The whole earth offers you prayer,
Clad in its white mantle of snow,
Sparkling like diamonds.
I have seen how the rising sun rejoices in you,
How the song of the birds is a chorus of praise to you.

I have heard the mysterious mutterings of the forests about you,
And the winds singing your praise as they stir the waters.
I have understood how the choirs of stars proclaim your glory
As they move for ever in the depths of infinite space.

You have brought me into life as if into an enchanted paradise.
We have seen the sky like a chalice of deepest blue,
Where in the heights the birds are singing.
We have listened to the soothing murmur of the forest
And the melodious music of the streams.
We have tasted fruit of fine flavor and sweet-scented honey.
We can live very well on your earth.
It is a pleasure to be your guest.
Glory to you for the feast-day of life.
Glory to you for the perfume of lilies and roses.
Glory to you for each different taste of berry and fruit.
Glory to you for the sparkling silver of early morning dew.
Glory to you for the joy of dawn's awakening.
Glory to you for the new life each day brings.
Glory to you O God, from age to age.

GREGORY PETROV

Awakening
in a moment of peace
I give thanks
to the source of all peace

as I set forth
into the day
the birds sing
with new voices
and I listen
with new ears
and give thanks

nearby
the flower called Angel's Trumpet
blows
in the breeze
and I give thanks

my feet touch the grass
still wet with dew
and I give thanks
both to my mother earth
for sustaining my steps
and to the seas
cycling once again
to bring forth new life

the dewdrops
become jewelled
with the morning's sun-fire
and I give thanks

you can see forever
when the vision is clear
in this moment
each moment
I give thanks

HARRIET KOFALK

Gratitude to Mother Earth, sailing through night and day—
and to her soil: rich, rare, and sweet
in our minds so be it

Gratitude to Plants, the sun-facing light-changing leaf
and fine root-hairs; standing still through wind
and rain; their dance is in the flowing spiral grain
in our minds so be it

Gratitude to Air, bearing the soaring Swift and the silent
Owl at dawn. Breath of our song
clear spirit breeze
in our minds so be it

Gratitude to Wild Beings, our brothers, teaching secrets,
freedoms, and ways; who share with us their milk;
self-complete, brave, and aware
in our minds so be it

Gratitude to Water: clouds, lakes, rivers, glaciers;
    holding or releasing; streaming through all
    our bodies salty seas
        in our minds so be it

Gratitude to the Sun: blinding pulsing light through
    trunks of trees, through mists, warming caves where
    bears and snakes sleep—he who wakes us—
        in our minds so be it

Gratitude to the Great Sky
    who holds billions of stars—and goes yet beyond that—
    beyond all powers, and thoughts
    and yet is within us—
    Grandfather Space.
    The Mind is his Wife.

        so be it.

        GARY SNYDER (AFTER A MOHAWK PRAYER)

We return thanks to our mother, the earth,
    which sustains us.
We return thanks to the rivers and streams,
    which supply us with water.
We return thanks to all herbs,
    which furnish medicines for the cure of our diseases.
We return thanks to the corn, and to her sisters,
    the beans and squashes,
    which give us life.
We return thanks to the wind,
    which, moving the air
    has banished diseases.
We return thanks to the moon and stars,
    which have given to us their light when the sun was gone.
We return thanks to the sun,
    that he has looked upon the earth with a beneficent eye.
Lastly, we return thanks to the Great Spirit,
    in whom is embodied all goodness,
    and who directs all things for the good of his children.

IROQUOIS PRAYER (ADAPTED)

We give-away our thanks to the earth
    which gives us our home.
We give-away our thanks to the rivers and lakes
    which give-away their water.
We give-away our thanks to the trees
    which give-away fruit and nuts.
We give-away our thanks to the wind
    which brings rain to water the plants.
We give-away our thanks to the sun
    who gives-away warmth and light.
All beings on earth: the trees, the animals, the wind
    and the rivers give-away to one another
    so all is in balance.
We give-away our promise to begin to learn
    how to stay in balance with all the earth.

DOLORES LA CHAPELLE

Behold! Our Mother Earth is lying here.
Behold! She gives of her fruitfulness.
Truly, her power she gives us.
Give thanks to Mother Earth who lies here.

Behold! On Mother Earth the growing fields!
Behold the promise of her fruitfulness!
Truly, her power she gives us.
Give thanks to Mother Earth who lies here.

Behold on Mother Earth the spreading trees!
Behold the promise of her fruitfulness!
Truly, her power she gives us.
Give thanks to Mother Earth who lies here.

Behold on Mother Earth the running streams;
We see the promise of her fruitfulness.
Truly, her power she gives us.
Our thanks to Mother Earth who lies here.

PAWNEE HAKO CEREMONY

i thank You God for most this amazing
day:for the leaping greenly spirits of trees
and a blue true dream of sky;and for everything
which is natural which is infinite which is yes

(i who have died am alive again today,
and this is the sun's birthday;this is the birth
day of life and of love and wings:and of the gay
great happening illimitably earth)

how should tasting touching hearing seeing
breathing any—lifted from the no
of all nothing—human merely being
doubt unimaginable You?

(now the ears of my ears awake and
now the eyes of my eyes are opened)

E. E. CUMMINGS

Waking up this morning, I see the blue sky
I join my hands in thanks for the many wonders of life;
    For having twenty-four brand new hours.
The sun is rising on the forest
    and so is my awareness.

I walk across the field of sunflowers.
Tens of thousands of flowers waving at me;
My awareness is like the sunflower;
My hands are sowing seeds for the next harvest.
My ear is hearing the sound of the rising tide on the magnificent
    sky.
I see clouds approaching with joy from many directions.
I can see the fragrant lotus ponds of my homeland;
I can see coconut trees along the rivers;
I can see rice fields stretch their shoulders
    laughing at the sun and the rain.
Mother Earth gives me coriander, basilicum, and celery.
Tomorrow, the hills and mountains of the country will be green
    again.
Tomorrow, the buds of life will grow quickly;
    the folk poetry will be as sweet as the songs of the children.
The whole family of humans will sing together with me in my
    work.

THICH NHAT HANH

All praise be yours through Brother Sun.
All praise be yours through Sister Moon.
By Mother Earth, the Spirit be Praised.
By Brother Mountain, Sister Sea
Through Brother Wind and Brother Air
Through Sister Water, Brother Fire
The Stars above give thanks to thee,
All praise to those who live in Peace.

All praise be yours, through Brother Wolf.
All praise be yours, through Sister Whale.
By nature's song, the spirit be praised.
By Brother Eagle, Sister Loon
Through Brother Tiger, Sister Seal,
Let creatures all give thanks to Thee.
All praise to those who live in peace.

Ask of the beasts and they shall teach you
the beauty of the Earth.
Ask of the Trees and they shall teach you
the beauty of the Earth.
Ask of the Flowers and they shall teach you
the beauty of the Earth.
Ask of the Wind and it shall teach you
the beauty of the Earth.

PAUL WINTER

Listen
with the night falling we are saying thank you
we are stopping on the bridges to bow from the railings
we are running out of the glass rooms
with our mouths full of food to look at the sky
and say thank you
we are standing by the water looking out
in different directions

back from a series of hospitals back from a mugging
after funerals we are saying thank you
after the news of the dead
whether or not we knew them we are saying thank you
looking up from tables we are saying thank you
in a culture up to its chin in shame
living in the stench it has chosen we are saying thank you

over telephones we are saying thank you
in doorways and in the backs of cars and in elevators
remembering wars and the police at the back door
and the beatings on stairs we are saying thank you
in the banks that use us we are saying thank you
with the crooks in office with the rich and fashionable
unchanged we go on saying thank you thank you

with the animals dying around us
our lost feelings we are saying thank you
with the forests falling faster than the minutes
of our lives we are saying thank you
with the words going out like cells of a brain
with the cities growing over us like the earth
we are saying thank you faster and faster
with nobody listening we are saying thank you
we are saying thank you and waving
dark though it is

W. S. MERWIN

VIII

BENEDICTION FOR
THE ANIMALS

> But ask now the beasts
> and they shall teach thee. . . .[1]

Animals, referred to by John Muir as our horizontal brothers, have long been recognized as essential to our development and well-being. Throughout history they have played a major role in human thought and culture. They inhabit our myths, fables, proverbs, and stories. There is a profound, inescapable need for animals among all peoples, for while animals have inhabited a world without people, we have never lived without the companionship, example, and practical help of animals.

Today, because of the wide-spread pollution of air and water, the rapid expansion of cities, and the destruction of wilderness habitat, we are seeing an imminent and irreversible loss of untamed animal life. We can only guess at the future effect on our children of living in a world in which elephants exist only in zoos, the great whales no longer fill the seas with their song, and the remaining forests are silent.

The fact that so many of us are increasingly isolated from the presence of animals may contribute to the growing despair we feel.

Direct encounter with animals, meeting them eye to eye on their own ground, evokes a sudden wonder and respect. Their vivid life brings us alive to the source that creates and sustains all beings. Without such encounters we risk losing that part of ourselves which most deeply resonates with nature—the heart of compassion.

> *In safety and in Bliss*
> *May all creatures be of a blissful heart.*[2]

If our greatest loss with the animals has been to lose touch with the reality of their existence, our second loss has been to banish them from our minds. We assume they have nothing to teach us about the predicaments of our existence. We no longer know how to listen to the wisdom of the various four-legged, six-legged, finned and winged creatures that share our life on this Earth. We forget they are ancestors as well as kindred. Long before we existed they worked out the round of life in thousands of variations, as though anticipating the experiments of human cultures.

In the following selection of Earth Prayers, our powers of empathy and compassion are called upon. We are asked to awaken to the plight of our animal relatives, to let their beauty and power come alive for us once more. We are members of a human family and society, but the presence of animal "others" enlarges our perception of the self beyond the city and opens us inward to that ground of being where live the lizard and monkey, the fish and the bear.

248

These are our relations. These are, like us, offspring of the great mystery, and necessary parts of a balanced and living whole.

---

[1]Job 12:7, KJV
[2]Sutta Nipata, 143–44

My paw is holy
herbs are everywhere
my paw
herbs are everywhere

My paw is holy
everything is holy
my paw
everything is holy

JAMES KOLLER

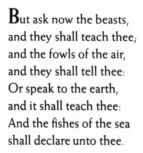

But ask now the beasts,
and they shall teach thee;
and the fowls of the air,
and they shall tell thee:
Or speak to the earth,
and it shall teach thee:
And the fishes of the sea
shall declare unto thee.

JOB 12:7–8, KJV

Out of the earth, I sing for them.
A horse nation, I sing for them.
Out of the earth, I sing for them.
The animals, I sing for them.

TETON SIOUX CHANT

Apprehend God in all things,
for God is in all things.

Every single creature is full of God
and is a book about God.

Every creature is a word of God.

If I spent enough time with the tiniest creature—
even a caterpillar—
I would never have to prepare a sermon. So full of God
is every creature.

MEISTER ECKHART

251

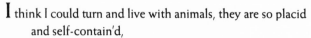

I think I could turn and live with animals, they are so placid
    and self-contain'd,
I stand and look at them long and long.

They do not sweat and whine about their condition,
They do not lie awake in the dark and weep for their sins,
They do not make me sick discussing their duty to God,
Not one is dissatisfied, not one is demented with the mania of
    owning things,
Not one kneels to another, nor to his kind that lived thousands
    of years ago,
Not one is respectable or unhappy over the whole earth.

               WALT WHITMAN

If I were alone in a desert
    and feeling afraid,
I would want a child to be with me.
For then my fear would disappear
    and I would be made strong.
This is what life in itself can do
because it is so noble, so full of pleasure
    and so powerful.
But if I could not have a child with me
I would like to have at least a living animal
at my side to comfort me.

Therefore,
let those who bring about wonderful things
in their big, dark books
take an animal
to help them.
The life within the animal
will give them strength in turn.
    For equality
gives strength, in all things
and at all times.

MEISTER ECKHART

Hear our humble prayer, O God, for our friends the animals, especially for animals who are suffering; for any that are hunted or lost, or deserted or frightened or hungry; for all that must be put to death. We entreat for them all thy mercy and pity and for those who deal with them we ask a heart of compassion and gentle hands and kindly words. Make us, ourselves, to be true friends to animals and so to share the blessings of the merciful.

ALBERT SCHWEITZER

Love animals: God has given them the rudiments of thought and joy untroubled. Do not trouble their joy, don't harass them, don't deprive them of their happiness, don't work against God's intent. Man, do not pride yourself on superiority to animals; they are without sin, and you, with your greatness, defile the earth by your appearance on it, and leave the traces of your foulness after you— alas, it is true of almost every one of us!

FYODOR DOSTOYEVSKY

O God, I thank thee
for all the creatures thou hast made,
so perfect in their kind—
great animals like the elephant and the rhinoceros,
humorous animals like the camel and the monkey,
friendly ones like the dog and the cat,
working ones like the horse and the ox,
timid ones like the squirrel and the rabbit,
majestic ones like the lion and the tiger,
for birds with their songs.
O Lord give us such love for thy creation,
that love may cast out fear,
and all thy creatures see in man
their priest and friend,
through Jesus Christ our Lord.

GEORGE APPLETON

You are singing, little dove,
on the branches of the silk-cotton tree.
And there also is the cuckoo,
and many other little birds.
All are rejoicing,
the songbirds of our god, our Lord.
And our goddess
has her little birds,
the turtledove, the redbird,
the black and yellow songbirds, and
    the hummingbird.
These are the birds of the beautiful
    goddess, our Lady.
If there is such happiness
among the creatures,
why do our hearts not also rejoice?
At daybreak all is jubilant.
Let only joy, only songs,
enter our thoughts!

SONG OF DZITBALCHE

We bless you, cicada,
high in the branches.
You sip a dew drop
and whistle like a king.
What you see is yours:
all the soft meadows
and furry mountains.
Yet you do no harm
in the farmer's field,
and men exalt you
as the voice of summer.
You are loved by Muses
and Apollo himself
who gave you clear song.
Wise child of the earth,
old age doesn't waste you.
Unfeeling and bloodless
you are like a god.

ANONYMOUS
HELLENISTIC POET

Elders

we have been here so short a time
and we pretend that we have invented memory

we have forgotten what it is like to be you
who do not remember us

we remember imagining that what survived us
would be like us

and would remember the world as it appears to us
but it will be your eyes that will fill with light

we kill you again and again
and we turn into you

eating the forests
eating the earth and the water

and dying of them
departing from ourselves

leaving you the morning
in its antiquity

W. S. MERWIN

258

It is neither spring nor summer: it is Always,
With towhees, finches, chickadees, California
    quail, wood doves,
With wrens, sparrows, juncos, cedar waxwings,
    flickers,
With Baltimore orioles, Michigan bobolinks,
And those birds forever dead,
The passenger pigeon, the great auk, the
    Carolina paraquet,
All birds remembered, O never forgotten!
All in my yard, of a perpetual Sunday,
All morning! All morning!

THEODORE ROETHKE

Their high pitched baying
as if in prayer's unison

remote, undistracted, given over
utterly to belief,

the skein of geese
voyages south,
        hierarchic arrow of its convergence toward
        the point of grace
swinging and rippling, ribbon tail
of a kite, loftily

over lakes where they have not
elected to rest,

over men who suppose
earth is man's, over golden earth

preparing itself
for night and winter.
                    We humans
are smaller than they, and crawl
unnoticed,

about and about the smoky map.

DENISE LEVERTOV

260

O my brothers of the wilderness,
My little brothers,
For my necessities
I am about to kill you!
May the Master of Life who made you
In the form of the quarry
That the children may be fed,
Speedily provide you
Another house;
So there may be peace
Between me and thy spirit.

MARY AUSTIN

Plants and Animals in the Garden,
We welcome you—we invite you in—we ask your forgiveness and
   your understanding. Listen as we invoke your names, as we
   also listen for you:

Little sparrows, quail, robins and house finches who have died in
   our strawberry nets;

Young Cooper's Hawk who flew into our sweet pea trellis and
   broke your neck;

Numerous orange-bellied newts who died by our shears, in our
   irrigation pipes, by our cars, and by our feet;

Slugs and snails whom we have pursued for years, feeding you to
   the ducks, crushing you, trapping you, picking you off and
   tossing you over our fences;

Gophers and moles, trapped and scorned by us, and also watched
   with love, admiration and awe for your one-mindedness;

Sowbugs, spitbugs, earwigs, flea beetles, woolly aphids, rose-
   suckers, cutworms, millipedes and other insects whom we
   have lured and stopped;

Snakes and moths who have been caught in our water system and
   killed by our mowers;

Families of mice who have died in irrigation pipes, by electricity
  in our pump box, and by predators while nesting in our
  greenhouses;
Manure worms and earthworms, severed by spades, and numerous
  microscopic lifeforms in our compost system who have been
  burned by sunlight;
Feral cats and raccoons whom we've steadily chased from the
  garden;
Rats whom we poisoned and trapped and drowned. Deer, chased
  at dawn and at midnight, routed by dogs, by farmers, by
  fences and numerous barriers;
Plants: colored lettuces, young broccoli, ripe strawberries and
  sweet apples, all of you who have lured the animals to your
  sides, and all plants we have shunned: poison hemlock,
  pigweed, bindweed, stinging nettle, bull thistle;
We call up plants we have removed by dividing you and separating
  you, and deciding you no longer grow well here;
We invoke you and thank you and continue to learn from you. We
  dedicate this ceremony to you. We will continue to practice
  with you and for you.

WENDY JOHNSON, GREEN GULCH FARM

And let me never,
Beholding providential food on the loot-loaded table,
Put out of my mind the great steer steaming in his own blood,
The hooks that haul him head-down and dripping,
Clinched in his hocks;
Nor hide the hurt of the soft calf,
New in the knowledge of his sudden doom;
Nor the hung hog;
Nor the lamb that looks at the suckering knife,
And cannot foresee;
Nor fowl;
Nor frog;
Nor down-diving fish on the line's treason—

    Was I not a fish?
    In the windless womb,
    In the Wilderness,
    Was I not frog?
    Turned I not in the turtle's torsion?
    Crept I not in the snail's span?

I hold at the heart,
At the timeless center,
All features,
All forms.
And wrung on the rack of what mutations,
This stringent flesh?

And let me never forget the tuber torn from its own fulfillment,
The globular wealth of genetic wheat
Crumbled to meal;
Nor forget the great horse hooked to the plough,
His generational strength nurtured thousands of years,
Sire to son,
For no profit of his.
Nor ever see fur on the shoulder of woman,
But mark how she paces,
Bright in the blood of a hundred miseries,
The pelt-plundered carcasses
Heaped on the balance her beauty breeds.

BROTHER ANTONINUS

Ah Power that swirls us together
Grant us Bliss
Grant us the great release
And to all Beings
Vanishing, wounded
In trouble on earth
We pass on this love
May their numbers increase.

GARY SNYDER

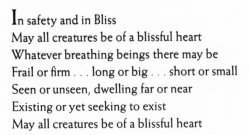

In safety and in Bliss
May all creatures be of a blissful heart
Whatever breathing beings there may be
Frail or firm . . . long or big . . . short or small
Seen or unseen, dwelling far or near
Existing or yet seeking to exist
May all creatures be of a blissful heart

SUTTA NIPATA, 143–52

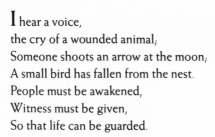

O God, scatterer of ignorance and darkness,
    grant me your strength.
May all beings regard me with the eye of a friend,
    and I all beings!
With the eye of a friend may each single being
    regard all others!

'SUKLA YAJUR, VEDA XXXVI

I hear a voice,
the cry of a wounded animal;
Someone shoots an arrow at the moon;
A small bird has fallen from the nest.
People must be awakened,
Witness must be given,
So that life can be guarded.

W. S. RENDRA

Let others pray for the passenger pigeon
the dodo, the whooping crane, the eskimo:
everyone must specialize

I will confine myself to a meditation
upon the giant tortoises
withering finally on a remote island.

I concentrate in subway stations,
in parks, I can't quite see them,
they move to the peripheries of my eyes

but on the last day they will be there;
already the event
like a wave travelling shapes vision:

on the road where I stand they will materialize,
plodding past me in a straggling line
awkward without water

their small heads pondering
from side to side, their useless armor
sadder than thanks and history,

in their closed gaze ocean and sunlight paralysed,
lumbering up the steps, under the archways
toward the square glass altars

where the brittle gods are kept,
the relics of what we have destroyed,
our holy and obsolete symbols.

MARGARET ATWOOD

The temple of the animals has fallen into disrepair.
The pad of feet has faded.
The panthers flee the shadows of the day.
The smell of musk has faded but lingers there . . .
lingers, lingers. Ah, bitterly in my room.
Tired, I recall the animals of last year:
the altars of the bear, tribunals of the ape,
solitudes of elephantine gloom, rare
zebra-striped retreats, prophecies of dog,
sanctuaries of the pygmy deer.

Were there rituals I had forgotten? Animal calls
to which those animal voices replied,
calld and calld until that jungle stirrd.
Were there voices that I heard?

Love was the very animal made his lair,
slept out his winter in my heart.
Did he seek my heart or ever
sleep there?

I have seen the animals depart,
forgotten their voices, or barely remembered
—like the last speech when the company
     goes
or the beloved face that the heart knows,
forgets and knows—
I have heard the dying footsteps fall.
The sound has faded, but lingers here.
Ah, bitterly I recall
the animals of last year.

ROBERT DUNCAN

You are the last whale,
washed up on a far beach.
The waves are pushing against you.
Your brothers and sisters are gone.
The light is too bright for your eyes.
You cannot breathe.
Small children are throwing rocks and laughing,
climbing onto your body.
You die alone, your ears full of wind.

You are the last buffalo.
The sun is setting over the plains.
You stand alone, enormous,
heavy with fur, lonely.
You are tired of running, tired of running.
All of your friends have gone.
It seems even the earth has turned against you.
There is not one to say goodbye.
You rest, listening to the wind.

> When the time is right,
>   the spirit of the wolf returns.

GARY LAWLESS

Grey Wolf
We are sending you
to that Great God.
Tell Him
That we, who invented forgiveness
do not forgive;
That we, who speak of trust
can not trust;
That we, who invoke faith would not believe.

I write as though you could read.
But I know you understand.
When you have left the forests and tundras
and no longer leave your sinewy trails within the snows,
    tell Him that
you were made on a different day.

Your howls of bewilderment will echo with the mountain
    winds.
And your songs will join those of the whales.
Tell Him for me,
"Forgive them Father for they know not what they do."

O. FRED DONALDSON

Here they are. The soft eyes open.
If they have lived in a wood
It is a wood.
If they have lived on plains
It is grass rolling
Under their feet forever.

Having no souls, they have come,
Anyway, beyond their knowing.
Their instincts wholly bloom
And they rise.
The soft eyes open.

To match them, the landscape flowers,
Outdoing, desperately
Outdoing what is required:
The richest wood,
The deepest field.

For some of these,
It could not be the place
It is, without blood.
These hunt, as they have done,
But with claws and teeth grown perfect,

More deadly than they can believe.
They stalk more silently,
And crouch on the limbs of trees,
And their descent
Upon the bright backs of their prey

May take years
In a sovereign floating of joy.
And those that are hunted
Know this as their life,
Their reward: to walk

Under such trees in full knowledge
Of what is in glory above them,
And to feel no fear,
But acceptance, compliance.
Fulfilling themselves without pain

At the cycle's center,
They tremble, they walk
Under the tree,
They fall, they are torn,
They rise, they walk again.

JAMES DICKEY

He thought he kept the universe alone;
For all the voice in answer he could wake
Was but the mocking echo of his own
From some tree-hidden cliff across the lake.
Some morning from the boulder-broken beach
He would cry out on life, that what it wants
Is not its own love back in copy speech,
But counter-love, original response.
And nothing ever came of what he cried
Unless it was the embodiment that crashed
In the cliff's talus on the other side,
And then in the far distant water splashed,
But after a time allowed for it to swim,
Instead of proving human when it neared
And someone else additional to him,
As a great buck it powerfully appeared,
Pushing the crumpled water up ahead,
And landed pouring like a waterfall,
And stumbled through the rocks with horny tread,
And forced the underbrush—and that was all.

ROBERT FROST

We ate no flesh in Eden, but afterwards,
when things got hard, we forgot
the peaceful kinship of that ancient kingdom.
As our teeth sank into their flesh
we had to deny them. So we said
they had no souls, no reason, no thumbs,
no speech. We were so different. We made
a chain of things to protect us—fire, medicine,
our locking houses, many kinds of clothes.
And we renamed them—farm product, fur crop,
renewable resource. Pray that we will see
their faces again in the mirror of creation,
the miracle of animals, their clear eyes
meaning more than profit to our own!

JEAN PEARSON

One way the world
could survive in joy
is if the whole world
worshipped whales.
If ancient Egyptians
worshipped cats,
how much more we
should worship whales!
I really believe
we should worship
the whales. &
regard them as
superior (if not
actually supreme)
intelligentsias

for they can nowise
hurt us. Unlike
most of the Gods
currently worshipped.
Their whole being
is exultation & play.
I believe we should
apprentice ourselves
to whales & dolphins
more eagerly than
to any human guru.
The whales sing &
play all day &
when they're hungry
all they do is open

their big mouths
(how can they help it
if millions of krill
happen to seep in).
Yes, the whales
sing & play all day
& don't have to mail
their songs to any
publisher whales
in order to be free
from factories & blow
geysers of ecstasy
all day long. The
whales have no factories
need no factories want
no factories & sing & play
& blow geysers of joy
all day. Their only
reason to go mad with
anguish & agony are
the lightning bolts
exploding unaccountably
into their brains,
harpoons expertly hurled
by beings made in image
of Jehovah—the explosive
harpoons of humanmind.
Aikido those harpoons,
most whale-like human friends.

JEFF PONIEWAZ

We hear you, fellow-creatures. We know we are wrecking the world and we are afraid. What we have unleashed has such momentum now, we don't know how to turn it around. Don't leave us alone, we need your help. You need us too for your own survival. Are there powers there you can share with us?

"I, lichen, work slowly, very slowly. Time is my friend. This is what I give you: patience for the long haul and perseverance."

"It is a dark time. As deep-diving trout I offer you my fearlessness of the dark."

"I, lion, give you my roar, the voice to speak out and be heard."

"I am caterpillar. The leaves I eat taste bitter now. But dimly I sense a great change coming. What I offer you, humans, is my willingness to dissolve and transform. I do that without knowing what the end-result will be; so I share with you my courage too."

JOANNA MACY

Little by little
roads eat away the hearts of mountains.
Fires burn through, come back in huckleberries,
trails close in August, too many bears.
Too many bears, now following avalanche chutes,
glacier lily, early spring.
Caribou in old growth spruce,
lichen,
banks of snow and fog.
Bear tracks in the mud.

Treat each bear as the last bear.
Each wolf as the last, each caribou.
Each track the last track,
Gone spoor. Gone scat.
There are no more deertrails,
no more flyways.
Treat each animal as sacred,
each minute our last.
Ghost hooves. Ghost skulls.
Death rattles and
dry bones.
Each bear walking alone
in warm night air.

GARY LAWLESS

IX

CYCLES OF LIFE

Spring, summer, autumn, winter—birth, growth, fading, death—the cycles of life turn, and we turn with them. Ideas are born, projects are consummated, plans prove impractical and die. We fall in love, we suffer loss; we give birth, we grow old. We are renewed, we are reborn, even as we decay and die. Our psychic energies are renewed in their deepest sources by this participation in the cycles of change within the natural world.

When we are aware of the Earth's processes, seeing ourselves as parts of a whole, we learn to let go of the need to control life. We are reminded to accept the inevitable cycles of green and dry, birth and death, cold and warm, emptiness and fullness, light and dark, that characterize the events and activities of our daily life. The prayers in this section draw us into this great seasonal round, reminding us of their role in shaping not only our physical existence but our human consciousness as well.

Just as the spring has been celebrated for tens of thousands of years as the point of fertility, as a time when nature displays its beauty to bring about the conception of new life, so too our own life has its birthing seasons.

> *As a newborn babe I crawl from my mother's womb*
> *And stand on wobbly legs in the new world;*
> *Wash the new body that has just been*
> *So tenderly born from a lifetime labor,*
> *And walk to stand before the fire.* [1]

With the summer solstice we feel the maximum power of the sun as it gives its fullest offering to our part of the Earth. The time of rigorous outward manifestation is here. Everywhere are the energies of doing. The garden image of summer applies to whatever we undertake; if we continue to give them our energies—sun, water, care, love—our dreams will grow and prosper. If we do not continue to nourish our dreams, they may wilt and perish.

Inevitably in every life there comes a time of waiting. In the fields the grain is ripe but not yet harvested. We have worked hard to bring things to fruition, but reward is not yet certain. The days shorten. We remember that to harvest we must sacrifice the warmth and light of summer and pass into autumn.

This is the time of harvest, of thanksgiving and of leavetaking and sorrow. Life appears to decline. The season of barrenness is upon us, yet we give thanks for that which we have reaped and gathered. The end of a cycle has come. We enter our resting season.

It is our quiet time.
We do not speak, because the voices are within us.
It is our quiet time.
We do not walk, because the earth is all within us.
It is our quiet time. . . .[2]

The seed now begins its time of gestation in the rich dark Earth. It is the great cold of night: not the negative images of darkness, but the dark richness of that unknown, fertile, deep part in each of us where our intuitive creative forces abide. The Christ energy enters the Earth at this season. The yule log is lighted. The nights grow shorter, the light returns, and we experience rebirth.

Again, again we come and go,
changed, changing. Hands
join, unjoin in love and fear,
grief and joy. The circles turn,
each giving into each, into all.[3]

[1]Rochelle Wallace
[2]Nancy Wood
[3]Wendell Berry

Within the circles of our lives
we dance the circles of the years,
the circles of the seasons
within the circles of the years,
the cycles of the moon
within the circles of the seasons,
the circles of our reasons
within the cycles of the moon.

Again, again we come and go,
changed, changing. Hands
join, unjoin in love and fear,
grief and joy. The circles turn,
each giving into each, into all.
Only music keeps us here,

each by all the others held.
In the hold of hands and eyes
we turn in pairs, that joining
joining each to all again.

And then we turn aside, alone,
out of the sunlight gone

into the darker circles of return.

WENDELL BERRY

To everything there is a season,
a time for every purpose under the sun:
A time to be born and a time to die;
a time to plant and a time to pluck up that which is planted;
a time to kill and a time to heal . . .
a time to weep and a time to laugh;
a time to mourn and a time to dance . . .
a time to embrace and a time to refrain from embracing;
a time to lose and a time to seek . . .
a time to rend and a time to sew;
a time to keep silent and a time to speak;
a time to love and a time to hate;
a time for war and a time for peace.

ECCLESIASTES 3:1–8, LAMSA.

To be of the Earth is to know
    the restlessness of being a seed
    the darkness of being planted
    the struggle toward the light
    the pain of growth into the light
    the joy of bursting and bearing fruit
    the love of being food for someone
    the scattering of your seeds
    the decay of the seasons
    the mystery of death
    and the miracle of birth.

JOHN SOOS

Rise up, my love, my fair one, and come away.

For lo, the winter is past, the rain is over *and* gone;

The flowers appear on the earth; the time of the singing *of birds* is
come, and the voice of the turtle is heard in our land;

The fig tree putteth forth her green figs, and the vines *with* the
tender grape give a *good* smell. Arise, my love, my fair one,
and come away.

O my dove, *that art* in the clefts of the rock, in the secret *places* of
the stairs, let me see thy countenance, let me hear thy voice;
for sweet *is* thy voice, and thy countenance *is* comely.

THE SONG OF SOLOMON 2:10–14, KJV

I'm filled with joy
when the day dawns quietly
over the roof of the sky.

Life was wonderful
in winter.
But did winter make me happy?
No, I always worried
about hides for boot-soles
and for boots;
and if there'd be enough
for all of us.
Yes, I worried constantly.

Life was wonderful
in summer.
But did summer make me happy?
No, I always worried
about reindeer skins and rugs for the platform.
Yes, I worried constantly.

Life was wonderful
when you stood at your fishing-hole
on the ice.
But was I happy waiting at my fishing hole?

No, I was always worried
for my little hook,
in case it never got a bite.
Yes, I worried constantly.

Life was wonderful
when you danced in the feasting-house.
But did this make me any happier?
No, I always worried
I'd forget my song.
Yes, I worried constantly.

Life was wonderful . . .
And I still feel joy
each time the day-break
whitens the dark sky
each time the sun
climbs over the roof of the sky.

ESKIMO SONG

291

Everywhere is the green of new growth,
The amazing sight of the renewal of the earth.
We watch the grass once again emerging from the ground.
We notice the bright green atop the dark green on the pine, the
    fir, the hemlock, the spruce, the cedar.
The alder is already in leaf.
The old plum trees still blossom, leaf and give forth fruit.
The locust is late as always.
Everywhere and always the song of birds . . . bees raiding the
    orchard, racoon prowling at nightfall, the earthworm
    tunneling the garden, chickens and rabbits pecking and
    nibbling, the goats tugging to reach new delights . . . all are
    the ubiquitous energies of life.

O Lord,
May we today be touched by grace, fascinated and moved by this
    your creation, energized by the power of new growth at work
    in your world.
May we move beyond viewing this life only through a frame, but
    touch it and be touched by it,
    know it and be known by it,
    love it and be loved by it.

May our bodies, our minds, our spirits, learn a new rhythm paced
    by the rhythmic pulse of the whole created order.
May spring come to us, be in us, and recreate life in us.

May we forge a new friendship with the natural world and
    discover a new affinity with beauty, with life, and with the
    Cosmic Christ in whom all things were created in heaven and
    on earth, visible or invisible, whether thrones or dominions
    or principalities or authorities . . . for all things were created
    through him and for him.
In his name.
Amen.

CHINOOK PSALTER

Lord of the springtime, Father of flower, field and fruit, smile on
us in these earnest days when the work is heavy and the toil
wearisome; lift up our hearts, O God, to the things worthwhile—
sunshine and night, the dripping rain, the song of the birds, books
and music, and the voices of our friends. Lift up our hearts to these
this night and grant us Thy peace. Amen.

W.E.B. DU BOIS

The extreme delicacy of this Easter morning
Spoke to me as a prayer and as a warning.
It was light on the brink, spring light
After a rain that gentled my dark night.
I walked through landscapes I had never seen
Where the fresh grass had just begun to green,
And its roots, watered deep, sprung to my tread;
The maples wore a cloud of feathery red,
But flowering trees still showed their clear design
Against the pale blue brightness chilled like wine.
And I was praying all the time I walked,
While starlings flew about, and talked, and talked.
Somewhere and everywhere life spoke the word.
The dead trees woke; each bush held its bird.
I prayed for delicate love and difficult,
That all be gentle now and know no fault,
That all be patient—as a wild rabbit fled
Sudden before me. Dear love, I would have said
(And to each bird who flew up from the wood),
I would be gentler still if that I could,
For on this Easter morning it would seem
The softest footfall danger is, extreme . . .

And so I prayed to be less than the grass
And yet to feel the Presence that might pass.
I made a prayer, I heard the answer, "Wait,
when all is so in peril, and so delicate!"

MAY SARTON

Over cherry blossoms
white clouds
over clouds
the deep sky

over cherry blossoms
over clouds
over the sky
I can climb on forever

once in spring
I with god
had a quiet talk.

SHUNTARO TANIKAWA

295

Through the weeks of deep snow
we walked above the ground
on fallen sky, as though we did
not come of root and leaf, as though
we had only air and weather
for our difficult home.

              But now
as March warms, and the rivulets
run like birdsong on the slopes,
and the branches of light sing in the hills,
slowly we return to earth.

WENDELL BERRY

Behold, my brothers, the spring has come;
The earth has received the embraces of the sun
And we shall soon see the results of that love!

Every seed is awakened and so has all animal life.
It is through this mysterious power that we too have our being
And we therefore yield to our neighbors,
Even our animal neighbors,
The same right as ourselves, to inhabit this land.

              SITTING BULL

A Light exists in Spring
Not present in the Year
At any other period—
When March is scarcely here

A Color stands abroad
on Solitary Fields
That Science cannot overtake
But Human Nature feels.

It waits upon the Lawn,
It shows upon the furthest Tree
Upon the furthest Slope you know
It almost speaks to you.

Then as Horizons step
Or Noons report away
Without the Formula of sound
It passes and we stay—

A quality of loss
Affecting our Content
As Trade had suddenly encroached
Upon a Sacrament.

EMILY DICKINSON

297

Ho! Sun, Moon, Stars, all that move in the heavens,
    I bid you hear me!
Into your midst has come a new life! Consent ye, I implore!
Make smooth its path that it may reach the brow of the first hill!

Ho! Winds, Clouds, Rain, Mist, all ye that move in the air,
    I bid you hear me!
Into your midst has come a new life! Consent ye, I implore!
Make smooth its path that it may reach the brow of the second
    hill!

Ho! Hills, Valleys, Rivers, Lakes, Trees, Grasses, all ye of the earth,
    I bid you hear me!
Into your midst has come a new life! Consent ye, I implore!
Make smooth its path that it may reach the brow of the third hill!

Ho! Birds great and small that fly in the air,
Ho! Animals great and small that dwell in the forest,
Ho! Insects that creep among the grasses and burrow in the
    ground—
    I bid you hear me!
Into your midst has come a new life! Consent ye, I implore!
Make its path smooth that it may reach the brow of the fourth hill!

Ho! All ye of the heavens, all ye of the air, all ye of the earth:
    I bid you all to hear me!

Into your midst has come a new life! Consent ye, consent ye all, I
    implore!
Make its path smooth—then shall it travel beyond the four hills!

OMAHA TRIBE PRAYER

Be praised, my God, by butterfly and dragonfly wings exercising
    for their first flight.

Be praised by lightning and thunder causing spring showers.

Be praised by the silent voice of grass growing and trees budding.

Be praised by all the colorful flower trumpets of spring.

Be praised by downy feathers freshly dried on newly hatched
    ducklings and chicks.

Be praised by the songs of birds, crickets and frogs.

Be praised, my God, by all your creation which tells of new life.

MARY GOERGEN, O.S.F.

To be sung by the one who first takes the child
 from its mother.

Newborn, on the naked sand
Nakedly lay it.
Next to the earth mother,
That it may know her;
Having good thoughts of her, the food giver.

Newborn, we tenderly
In our arms take it,
Making good thoughts.
House-god, be entreated,
That it may grow from childhood to manhood,
Happy, contented;
Beautifully walking
The trail to old age.
Having good thoughts of the earth its mother,
That she may give it the fruits of her being.
Newborn, on the naked sand
Nakedly lay it.

GRANDE PUEBLOS SONG

300

As a newborn babe I crawl from my mother's womb
And stand on wobbly legs in the new world;
Wash the new body that has just been
So tenderly born from a lifetime labor,
And walk to stand before the fire.
I raise my face to your infinite sky
And feel your touch of grace:
Your gentle raindrops kissing my skin,
Your singing wind that moves the trees,
The hot breath of your dancing fire,
Your wet, rich earth beneath my feet.
O Spirit, I recognize you now:
My father, my mother, my unseen lover—
You've been here always in all things;
In all things has your spirit lived for me;
From all things has your spirit loved me.
Through all things has your spirit touched me.
And never was I left alone, nor could I be
In this truer world of holy people
And living stone.

ROCHELLE WALLACE

Flowers have come!
    to refresh
    and delight you, princes.

You see them briefly
as they dress themselves,
spread their petals,
perfect only in spring—
countless golden flowers!

The flowers have come
to the skirt of the mountain!

Yellow flowers
sweet flowers

precious vanilla flowers
the crows dark magic flowers

weave themselves together.

They are your
flowers, god.

We only borrow them:
your flowered drum,
your bells,
your song:

They are your flowers,
god.

NEZAHUALCOYOTL

I offer flowers. I sow flower seeds. I plant flowers. I assemble flowers. I pick flowers. I pick different flowers. I remove flowers. I seek flowers. I offer flowers. I arrange flowers. I thread a flower. I string flowers. I make flowers. I form them to be extending, uneven, rounded, round bouquets of flowers.

I make a flower necklace, a flower garland, a paper of flowers, a bouquet, a flower shield, hand flowers. I thread them. I string them. I provide them with grass. I provide them with leaves. I make a pendant of them. I smell something. I smell them. I cause one to smell something. I cause him to smell. I offer flowers to one. I offer him flowers. I provide him with flowers. I provide one with flowers. I provide one with a flower necklace. I provide him with a flower necklace. I place a garland on one. I provide him with a garland. I clothe one in flowers. I cover him in flowers. I love him with flowers.

AZTEC SONG

as my eyes
search
the prairie
I feel the summer
in the spring

CHIPPEWA SONG

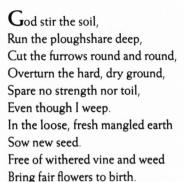

God stir the soil,
Run the ploughshare deep,
Cut the furrows round and round,
Overturn the hard, dry ground,
Spare no strength nor toil,
Even though I weep.
In the loose, fresh mangled earth
Sow new seed.
Free of withered vine and weed
Bring fair flowers to birth.

PRAYER FROM SINGAPORE,
CHURCH MISSIONARY SOCIETY

Be a gardener.
Dig a ditch,
toil and sweat,
and turn the earth upside down
and seek the deepness
and water the plants in time.
Continue this labor
and make sweet floods to run
and noble and abundant fruits
to spring.
Take this food and drink
and carry it to God
as your true worship.

JULIAN OF NORWICH

Sowing the seed,
my hand is one with the earth.

Wanting the seed to grow,
my mind is one with the light.

Hoeing the crop,
my hands are one with the rain.

Having cared for the plants,
my mind is one with the air.

Hungry and trusting,
my mind is one with the earth.

Eating the fruit,
my body is one with the earth.

WENDELL BERRY

I thirst by day. I watch by night.
I receive! I have been received!
I hear the flowers drinking in their light,
I have taken counsel of the crab and the sea-urchin,
I recall the falling of small waters,
The stream slipping beneath the mossy logs,
Winding down to the stretch of irregular sand,
The great logs piled like matchsticks.

I am most immoderately married:
The Lord God has taken my heaviness away:
I have merged, like the bird, with the bright air,
And my thought flies to the place by the bo-tree.

Being, not doing, is my first job.

THEODORE ROETHKE

O Kané! Transform the earth
Let the earth move as in one piece
The land is cracked and fissured

The edible ferns yet grow, O Lono
Let kupukupu cover the dry lands
Gather potatoes as stones on the hills
The rain comes like the side of cliffs
The rain falling from Heaven
The potato falls from the heavens
The wild taro is only taro now
The taro of the mountain patches
The only food is that of the wilds
O Kané
O Kané and Lono! Gods of the husbandmen
Give life to the land
Until the food goes to waste
Until it sprouts in the ground
Until the leaves cover the land;
And such be plenty
Of you, Kané and Lono
The burden is lifted, we are free.

ANCIENT HAWAIIAN HEALING CHANT

The garden is rich with diversity
With plants of a hundred families
In the space between the trees
With all the colours and fragrances.
Basil, mint and lavender,
God keep my remembrance pure,
Raspberry, Apple, Rose,
God fill my heart with love,
Dill, anise, tansy,
Holy winds blow in me.
Rhododendron, zinnia,
May my prayer be beautiful
May my remembrance O God
    be as incense to thee
In the sacred grove of eternity
As I smell and remember
The ancient forests of earth.

CHINOOK PSALTER

August.
The opposing
of peach and sugar,
and the sun inside the afternoon
like the stone in the fruit.

The ear of corn keeps
its laughter intact, yellow and firm.

August.
The little boys eat
brown bread and delicious moon.

FEDERICO GARCIA LORCA

Many poplars and many elms shook overhead,
and close by, holy water swashed down noisily
from a cave of the nymphs. Brown grasshoppers
whistled busily through the dark foliage. Far
treetoads gobbled in the heavy thornbrake.

Larks and goldfinch sang, turtledoves were moaning,
and bumblebees whizzed over the splashing brook.

The earth smelled of rich summer and autumn fruit:
we were ankle-deep in pears, and apples rolled
all about our toes. With dark damson plums
the young sapling branches trailed on the ground.

THEOKRITOS

I ask for a moment's indulgence to sit by Thy side.
The works that I have in hand
I will finish afterwards.

Away from the sight of Thy face
My heart knows no rest or respite,
And my work becomes an endless toil
In a shoreless sea of toil.

Today the summer has come at my window
With its sighs and murmurs;
And the bees are plying their minstrelsy
At the court of the flowering grove.

Now it is time to sit quiet
Face to face with Thee,
And to sing dedication of life
In this silent and overflowing leisure.

RABINDRANATH TAGORE

Lord, it is time. The summer was very big.
Lay thy shadow on the sundials,
and on the meadows let the winds go loose.

Command the last fruits that they shall be full;
give them another two more southerly days,
press them on to fulfillment and drive
the last sweetness into the heavy wine.

Who has no house now, will build him one no more.
Who is alone now, long will so remain,
will wake, read, write long letters
and will in the avenues to and fro
restlessly wander, when the leaves are blowing.

RAINER MARIA RILKE

O sacred season of Autumn, be my teacher,
    for I wish to learn the virtue of contentment.
As I gaze upon your full-colored beauty,
    I sense all about you
    an at-homeness with your amber riches.

You are the season of retirement,
    of full barns and harvested fields.
The cycle of growth has ceased,
    and the busy work of giving life
    is now completed.
I sense in you no regrets:
    you've lived a full life.

I live in a society that is ever-restless,
    always eager for more mountains to climb,
    seeking happiness through more and more possessions.
As a child of my culture,
    I am seldom truly at peace with what I have.
Teach me to take stock of what I have given and received;
    may I know that it's enough,
    that my striving can cease
    in the abundance of God's grace.
May I know the contentment
    that allows the totality of my energies
    to come to full flower.

May I know that like you I am rich beyond measure.

As you, O Autumn, take pleasure in your great bounty,
    let me also take delight
    in the abundance of the simple things in life
    which are the true source of joy.
With the golden glow of peaceful contentment
    may I truly appreciate this autumn day.

EDWARD HAYS

The moon is full, the autumn nights grow longer,
In the north forests startled crows cry out.
Still high overhead, the star river stretches,
The Dipper's handle set to southwest.
The cold cricket grieves deep in the chambers,
Of the notes of sweet birds, none remain.
Then one evening gusts of autumn come,
One who sleeps alone thinks fondly on thick quilts.
Past loves are a thousand miles farther each day,
Blocked from my drifting and my sinking.
Man's life is not as the grass and trees;
Still the season's changes can stir the heart.

WEI YING WU

Green leaves
That dawn after dawn
Grow yellow;
Red cheeks
That fade
With the passing days—
If our world
Is made up
Of such changes
As these,
Is it strange
That my heart
Is so sad?

HSIAO KANG

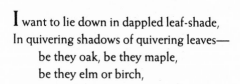

I want to lie down in dappled leaf-shade,
In quivering shadows of quivering leaves—
    be they oak, be they maple,
    be they elm or birch,

I want to rest in the play of shadows
    over my reclining form,
The massage of shadows
    which consoles me in its way,
Restores for me
    with whatever restoration
Flickering shadows of leaves afford—
    be they willow or aspen,
    be they poplar or beech,
I want to be caressed by shadows
    of wavering leaves,
Soothed off to sleep
    feeling the gentle breeze,
Looking up at the rustling
    sun-drenched crown—
Be it basswood, be it chestnut,
Be it walnut or hickory,
    after all is said,
    after all is done,
This is the way
I would die.

ANTLER

I walk in your world
a mercy, a healing—

Like a cooper of barrels
you bind the mountains with ribbing
your hand rests on rambunctious seas
they grow peaceful
        the brow of a sleeping child

Autumn is a king's progress
        largesse lies ripe on the land

up, down the furrow your midas touch
rains gold;
        rainbows are from your glance

Fall of rain, evenfall, all all is blessing!

DANIEL BERRIGAN

One leaf left on a branch
and not a sound of sadness
or despair. One leaf left
on a branch and no unhappiness.
One leaf left all by itself
in the air and it does not speak
of loneliness or death.
One leaf and it spends itself
in swaying mildly in the breeze.

DAVID IGNATOW

Clouds and mountains all tangled together up to the blue sky
a rough road and deep woods without any travellers
far away the lone moon a bright glistening white
nearby a flock of birds sobbing like children
one old man sitting alone   perched in these green mountains
a small shack   the retired life   letting my hair grow white
pleased with the years gone by   happy with today
mindless this life is like water flowing east

HAN-SHAN

319

That time of year thou mayst in me behold
When yellow leaves, or none, or few, do hang
Upon those boughs which shake against the cold,
Bare ruined choirs where late the sweet birds sang.
In me thou see'st the twilight of such day
As after sunset fadeth in the west,
Which by and by black night doth take away,
Death's second self, that seals up all in rest.
In me thou see'st the glowing of such fire
That on the ashes of his youth doth lie,
As the deathbed whereon it must expire,
Consumed with that which it was nourished by.
    This thou perceiv'st, which makes thy love more strong,
    To love that well which thou must leave ere long.

WILLIAM SHAKESPEARE

Cold, Cold,
Frost, Frost,
Fling me not aside!
You have bent me enough.
Away! Away!

320   AIVILIK ESKIMO CHANT

The longer we are together
the larger death grows around
    us.
How many we know by now
who are dead! We, who were
    young,
now count the cost of having
    been.
And yet as we know the dead
we grow familiar with the
    world.
We, who were young and loved
    each other
ignorantly, now come to know
each other in love, married
by what we have done, as
    much
as by what we intend. Our hair
turns white with our ripening
as though to fly away in some
coming wind, bearing the seed
of what we know. It was bitter
    to learn
that we come to death as we
    come
to love, bitter to face
the just and solving welcome
that death prepares. But that is
    bitter
only to the ignorant, who pray
it will not happen. Having
    come
the bitter way to better prayer,
    we have
the sweetness of ripening.
    How sweet
to know you by the signs of the
    world!

WENDELL BERRY

To learn how to die cut down a tree,
Watch how so many years fall.
You don't need to have planted it for it to be your life.

You know countless trees have grown
  and will grow where this tree falls
Everyone alive now will be underground
  and will have gone from roots, branches and leaves
    to roots, branches and leaves many times.
You've seen how the seed of a tree
  can rise from the pit of a stump.
Wherever your feet touch earth
  you know you are touching
    where something has died or been born.

Count the rings and stand on the stump and stretch your arms
  to the sky.
Think only because it was cut down could you do this.
You are standing where no one has stood
  but the dark inside a life
    that many years.

ANTLER

Mother of my birth, for how long were we together
in your love and my adoration of your self?
For the shadow of a moment, as I breathed your pain
and you breathed my suffering. As we knew
of shadows in lit rooms that would swallow the light.

Your face beneath the oxygen tent was alive
but your eyes closed, your breathing hoarse.
Your sleep was with death. I was alone
with you as when I was young
but now only alone, not with you,
to become alone forever, as I was learning
watching you become alone.
Earth now is your mother, as you were mine, my earth,
my sustenance and my strength,
and now without you I turn to your mother
and seek from her that I may meet you again
in rock and stone. Whisper to the stone
I love you. Whisper to the rock, I found you.
Whisper to the earth, Mother, I have found her,
and I am safe and always have been.

DAVID IGNATOW

It is our quiet time.
We do not speak, because the voices are within us.
It is our quiet time.
We do not walk, because the earth is all within us.
It is our quiet time.
We do not dance, because the music has lifted us to a place where
        the spirit is.
It is our quiet time.
We rest with all of nature. We wake when the seven sisters wake.
We greet them in the sky over the opening of the kiva.

NANCY WOOD

Could it be true we live on earth?
On earth forever?

Just one brief instant here.

Even the finest stones begin to split,
even gold is tarnished,
even precious bird-plumes
shrivel like a cough.

Just one brief instant here.

NEZAHUALCOYOTL

Life and death,
a twisted vine sharing a single root.

A water bright green
stretching to top a twisted yellow
only to wither itself
as another green unfolds overhead.

One leaf atop another
yet under the next;
a vibrant tapestry of arcs and falls
all in the act of becoming.

Death is the passing of life.
And life
is the stringing together of so many little passings.

RABBI RAMI M. SHAPIRO

How shall the mighty river
reach the tiny seed?
See it rise silently
to the sun's yearning,
sail from a winter's cloud
flake after silent flake
piling up layer upon layer
until the thaw of spring
to meet the seedling's need.

Make tender, Lord, my heart:
release through gentleness
Thine own tremendous power
hid in the snowflake's art.

ANTOINETTE ADAM

All winter long
behind every thunder
guess what we heard!
—behind every thunder
the song
of a bird,
a trumpeting bird.

All winter long
beneath every snowing
guess what we saw!
—beneath every snowing
a thaw
and a growing,
a greening and growing.

Where did we run
beyond gate and guardsman?
Guess, if you can!
—all winter long
we ran
to the sun,
the dance of the sun!

NATIVE AMERICAN SONG

In February
All of a sudden there's a lot more light
And it's a warm light—snow melts off the roof,
The first lambs are born in the barn cellar,
The hens start laying, the mare comes into season,
And I notice that the geraniums at the window
Have pushed their stalks up eight inches
And covered them with brick-pink blossoms.

Every day I wake up earlier
And my bones crack as I sit up and stretch.
When I poke my boot through a drift in the field
I find clover growing green beneath it.
Now the sap is running
And when I drive my sleigh up to the wood lot
I see three young maple bushes
Deeply scored with new bear scratches.

Oh warm light,
Couldn't you have waited a little longer?
How safe we were in the dead of winter,
How gently we dreamed,
How beautiful it was to sleep under the snow!

KATE BARNES

Again did the
earth shift.
Again did the
nights grow
short,
And the days long

And the people
of the earth
were glad
and celebrated
each in their
own ways

DIANE LEE MOOMEY

Far away in the depth of the mountains
Wandering here and there I carry no thought
When spring comes I watch the birds;
In summer I bathe in the running stream;
In autumn I climb the highest peaks;
During the winter I am warming up in the sun
Thus I enjoy the real flavor of the seasons

SHIH T'AO

X

THE DAILY
ROUND

ULTIMATELY, EARTH PRAYER
is about relationship, about returning to a vivid, nourishing relation
with the cosmos. One way to do that is through daily ritual. We
can once again practice the rituals of dawn and noon and sunset.
The rituals of lighting the lamp and pouring water, the rituals of
first breath and last. Imagine people waking and rising together and
beginning by singing themselves—body, mind and spirit—into
the day. The next thought they hold in common is loving goodwill
toward all living things. For thousands of years our ancestors have
done just this.

> *A new day needs to be honored.*
> *People have always known that.*
> *Didn't they chant at dawn in the sun temples of Peru?*
> *And leap and sway to Aztec flutes in Mexico?*
> *And drum sunrise songs in the Congo?*
> *And ring a thousand small gold bells in China?*[1]

As physical exercise makes our bodies robust, daily spiritual
practice awakens our latent inner powers, and we soon find our own
voice. Our own daily Earth Prayers may have no words, just a

prayer of the heart as we dedicate a piece of work, or bless the beings that give us our food or our water. It is not the words, but the state of mind evoked by our praying, which is potent.

This chapter is divided into four sections. Each section is composed of prayers and poems which call us to awareness at key moments throughout our day. We often become so busy that we forget what we are doing or why we are doing it. Pausing to praise the dawn or to bless our meal brings us into the present. It helps us to see the meaning and value of each precious moment of our life.

Another way to help us dwell in the present moment is to call to mind *gathas,* or inspirational verses. These little prayers help us to focus our attention and heighten our awareness of each activity. The ones in this book are only suggestions—signposts pointing us toward the poetic art of creating our own brief verses to accompany our daily activities.

Through these rituals, powerful energies flow into the world. As we mark the daily round with our prayers, we take our place in the grand liturgy of the cosmos.

And now I wish to pray and perform
a ritual of my devotion to the sun.
I will bow and sing beneath my breath,
then perform the dance of farewell
and my confidence in the sun's return.[2]

[1]Byrd Baylor
[2]David Ignatow

GREETING THE DAY

A sound arises out of the earth—
a singing, a friendliness.

CEDRIC WRIGHT

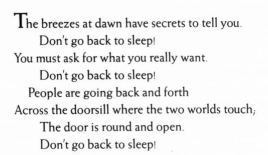

The breezes at dawn have secrets to tell you.
    Don't go back to sleep!
You must ask for what you really want.
    Don't go back to sleep!
  People are going back and forth
Across the doorsill where the two worlds touch;
    The door is round and open.
    Don't go back to sleep!

334   RUMI

With all of mankind, towards the light.

I shall raise the children
High, high, laughing for joy to the sun.

YANG LIAN

The sunbeams stream forward, dawn boys,
with shimmering shoes of yellow.

MESCALERO APACHE SONG

Waking up this morning, I smile,
Twenty four brand new hours are before me.
I vow to live fully in each moment
and to look at all beings with eyes of compassion.

THICH NHAT HANH

The day has risen,
Go I to behold the dawn,
Hao! you maidens!
Go behold the dawn!
The white-rising!
The yellow-rising!
It has become light.

HOPI SONG

Day arises
From its sleep,
Day wakes up
With the dawning light.
Also you must arise,
Also you must awake
Together with the day which comes.

THULE ESKIMO SONG

I arise from rest with movements swift
As the beat of a raven's wings
I arise
To meet the day
Wa-wa.
My face is turned from the dark of night
To gaze at the dawn of day,
Now whitening in the sky.

IGLULIK ESKIMO SONG

I arise, facing East,
I am asking toward the light;
I am asking that my day
Shall be beautiful with light.
I am asking that the place
Where my feet are shall be light,
That as far as I can see
I shall follow it aright.
I am asking for the courage
To go forward through the shadow,
I am asking toward the light!

MARY AUSTIN

When you arise in the morning,
give thanks for the morning light,
for your life and strength.
Give thanks for your food
and the joy of living.

If you see no reason for giving thanks,
the fault lies in yourself.

TECUMSEH

Morning has broken like the first morning,
Blackbird has spoken like the first bird.
Praise for the singing! Praise for the morning!
Praise for them springing fresh from the Word.

Sweet the rain's new fall sunlit from heaven,
Like the first dewfall on the first grass.
Praise for the sweetness of the wet garden,
Sprung in completeness where His feet pass.

Mine is the sunlight! Mine is the morning!
Born of the one light Eden saw play.
Praise with elation, praise every morning,
God's recreation of the new day!

ELEANOR FARJEAN

The heavens bespeak the glory of God.
The firmament ablaze, a text of his works.
Dawn whispers to sunset
Dark to dark the word passes; glory glory.

All in a great silence,
no tongue's clamor—
yet the web of the world trembles
conscious, as of great winds passing.

The bridegroom's tent is raised,
a cry goes up: He comes! a radiant sun
rejoicing, presiding, his wedding day.
From end to end of the universe his progress.
No creature, no least being but catches fire from him.

DANIEL BERRIGAN

Great mystery of sleep,
Which has safely brought us to the beginning of this day
We thank you for the refreshment you daily provide,
And for the renewing cycle of your dreams
Which shelter our fantasies, nourish our vision,
    and purge our angers and fears.
We bless you for providing a new beginning
Whose perennial grace is tangible hope
    for all the children of earth.
We praise the gift of another morning,
And pray that we may be worthy bearers of its trust
    in the hours to come.
May life protect us and surprise us
And be no more harsh than our spirits may bear
Until we rest again in the vast emptiness
    of your everlasting arms. Amen.

CONGREGATION OF ABRAXAS

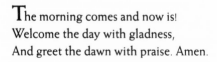

The morning comes and now is!
Welcome the day with gladness,
And greet the dawn with praise. Amen.

CONGREGATION OF ABRAXAS

Earth our mother, breathe forth life
    all night sleeping
    now awaking
    in the east
    now see the dawn

Earth our mother, breathe and waken
    leaves are stirring
    all things moving
    new day coming
    life renewing

Eagle soaring, see the morning
    see the new mysterious morning
    something marvelous and sacred
    though it happens every day
    Dawn the child of God and Darkness

        PAWNEE PRAYER

O Lord,
I am caught in that moment of half-light,
the breathless point of balance between sun and moon.
As I bid farewell to the cold purification of the night,
in that same movement, I fling wide my arms
to be embraced by the warmth and glory of the sun,
knowing that in due time I will bow to the receding light
and open my arms to darkness once again.

Thus, O Lord, You come into our lives,
in the blaze of splendour, the certainty of Your presence,
in the times of aridity and isolation, even to the point of
        despair.
Throughout this continuing journeying,
from the zenith of midday to the depths of midnight
and back to blinding noontide, we grow towards You,
the true light, that shines like the sun beyond darkness,
        forever.

ISHPRIYA R.S.C.J.

Listen to the salutation to the dawn,
Look to this day for it is life, the very life of life,
In its brief course lie all the verities and realities of our
existence.

The bliss of growth, the splendour of beauty,
For yesterday is but a dream and tomorrow is only a
    vision,
But today well spent makes every yesterday a dream
    of happiness
    and every tomorrow a vision of hope.
Look well therefore to this day.
Such is the salutation to the dawn.

SANSKRIT SALUTATION TO THE DAWN

A certain day became a presence to me;
there it was, confronting me—a sky, air, light:
a being. And before it started to descend
from the height of noon, it leaned over
and struck my shoulder as if with
the flat of a sword, granting me
honor and a task. The day's blow
rang out, metallic—or it was I, a bell awakened,
and what I heard was my whole self
saying and singing what it knew: I can.

DENISE LEVERTOV

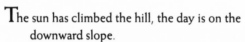

The sun has climbed the hill, the day is on the
    downward slope.
Between the morning and the afternoon, stand I here
    with my soul, and lift it up.
My soul is heavy with sunshine, and steeped with
    strength.
The sunbeams have filled me like a honeycomb,
It is the moment of fulness,
And the top of the morning.

D.H. LAWRENCE

GRACES

Earth, water, air, and fire combined to make this food.
Numberless beings have died and labored that we may eat.
May we be nourished that we may nourish life.

OJAI SCHOOL

The food which we are about to eat
Is Earth, Water, and Sun, compounded through the alchemy
    of many plants.
Therefore Earth, Water and Sun will become part of us.
This food is also the fruit of the labor of many beings and
    creatures.
We are grateful for it.

May it give us strength, health, joy.

And may it increase our love.

UNITARIAN PRAYER

Food is not matter
but the heart of matter,
the flesh and blood of
rock and water, earth and sun.

Food is not a commodity
which price can capture,
but exacting effort,
carefully sustained,
the life work of countless
beings.

With this cooking I enter
the heart of matter,
I enter the intimate activity
which makes dreams materialize.

EDWARD ESPE BROWN

346

May the Ocean of Salt, the Ocean of
Honey, the Ocean of Wine, the Ocean
of Ghee, the Ocean of Curd, the
Ocean of Milk, the Ocean of Sweet
Water sprinkle thee with their
consecrated waters.

MAHANIRVANA TANTRA X

We venerate the Three Treasures:
Buddha, Dharma, Sangha,
And are thankful for this meal,
The work of many people
And the sharing of other forms of life.

ZEN PRAYER

Looking at Your Empty Plate:
    My plate, empty now,
    will soon be filled
    with precious food.

Looking at Your Full Plate:
    In this food,
    I see clearly the presence
    of the entire universe
    supporting my existence.

Contemplating Your Food:
    This plate of food,
    so fragrant and appetizing,
    also contains much suffering.

Beginning to Eat:

    With the first taste, I promise to offer joy.

    With the second, I promise to help relieve
        the suffering of others.

    With the third, I promise to see others' joy
        as my own.

    With the fourth, I promise to learn the way
        of non-attachment and equanimity.

Finishing Your Meal:

    The plate is empty.
    My hunger is satisfied.
    I vow to live
    for the benefit of all beings.

Washing the Dishes:

    Washing the dishes
    is like bathing a baby Buddha.
    The profane is the sacred.
    Everyday mind is Buddha's mind.

THICH NHAT HANH

Our father, hear us, and our grandfather. I mention also all those that shine, the yellow day, the good wind, the good timber, and the good earth.

All the animals, listen to me under the ground. Animals above ground, and water animals, listen to me. We shall eat your remnants of food. Let them be good.

Let there be long breath and life. Let the people increase, the children of all ages, the girls and the boys, and the men of all ages and the women, the old men of all ages and the old women. The food will give us strength whenever the sun runs.

Listen to us, Father, Grandfather. We ask thought, heart, love, happiness. We are going to eat.

ARAPAHO GRACE

Eternal Spirit of Justice and Love,
At this time of Thanksgiving we would be aware of our
dependence on the earth and on the sustaining presence of other
human beings both living and gone before us.

As we partake of bread and wine, may we remember that
there are many for whom sufficient bread is a luxury, or for whom
wine, when attainable, is only an escape. Let our thanksgiving for
Life's bounty include a commitment to changing the world, that
those who are now hungry may be filled and those without hope
may be given courage.

Amen.

CONGREGATION OF ABRAXAS

I'm an Indian
I think about common things like this pot.
The bubbling water comes from the rain cloud.
It represents the sky.
The fire comes from the sun
which warms us all, men, animals, trees.
The meat stands for the four-legged creatures,
our animal brothers,
who gave of themselves so that we should live.
The steam is living breath.
It was water, now it goes up to the sky,
becomes a cloud again.
These things are sacred.
Looking at that pot full of good soup,
I am thinking how, in this simple manner,
The great Spirit takes care of me.

JOHN LAME DEER

Eating the living germs of grasses
Eating the ova of large birds

> the fleshy sweetness packed
> around the sperm of swaying trees

The muscles of the flanks and thighs of soft-voiced cows
> the bounce in the lamb's leap
> the swish in the ox's tail

Eating roots grown swoll
> inside the soil

Drawing on life of living
> clustered points of light spun
>> out of space
hidden in the grape.

Eating each other's seed
> eating
> ah, each other.

Kissing the lover in the mouth of bread:
> lip to lip.

GARY SNYDER

353

My friends, let us give thanks for Wonder.
Let us give thanks for the Wonder of Life
that infuses all things now and forever.

Blessed is the Source of Life, the Fountain of Being
the wellspring of goodness, compassion and kindness
from which we draw to make for justice and peace.
From the creative power of Life we derive food and harvest,
from the bounty of the earth and the yields of the heavens
we are sustained and are able to sustain others.
All Life is holy, sacred,
worthy of respect and dignity.
Let us give thanks for the power of heart
to sense the holy in the midst of the simple.

We eat not simply to satisfy our own appetites,
we eat to sustain ourselves in the task we have been given.
Each of us is unique,
coming into the world with a gift no other can offer: ourselves.
We eat to nourish the vehicle of giving,
we eat to sustain our task of world repair,
our quest for harmony, peace and justice.

We eat and we are revived, and we give thanks
to the lives that were ended to nourish our own.
May we merit their sacrifice, and honor their sparks of holiness
through our deeds of loving kindness.

We give thanks to the Power that makes for Meeting,
for our table has been a place of dialogue and friendship.

We give thanks to Life.
May we never lose touch with the simple joy and wonder
of sharing a meal.

RABBI RAMI M. SHAPIRO

At Candlelighting:
    May this Sabbath
    lift our spirits,
    lighten our hearts.

Sanctification over Wine:
    Let us bless the source of life
    that ripens fruit on the vine
    as we hallow the Sabbath day
    in remembrance of creation.

Washing the Hands:
    Washing the hands, we call to mind
    the holiness of the body.

Blessing over Bread:
    Let us bless the source of life
    that brings forth bread from the earth.

Blessing after the Meal:
    Let us acknowledge the source of life
    for the earth and for nourishment.
    May we protect the earth
    that it may sustain us,
    and let us seek sustenance
    for all who inhabit the world.

MARCIA FALK, PRAYER FOR THE SABBATH

By what miracle
does this cracker
made from Kansas wheat,
this cheese ripened in French caves,
this fig, grown and dried near Ephesus,
turn into Me?
My eyes,
My hands,
My cells, organs, juices, thoughts?

Am I not then Kansas wheat
and French cheese
and Smyrna figs?
Figs, no doubt,
the ancient Prophets ate?

JUDITH MORLEY

357

Blessed be the Creator
and all creative hands
which plant and harvest,
pack and haul and hand
over sustenance—
Blessed be carrot and cow,
potato and mushroom,
tomato and bean,
parsley and peas,
onion and thyme,
garlic and bay leaf,
pepper and water,
marjoram and oil,
and blessed be fire—
and blessed be the enjoyment
of nose and eye,
and blessed be color—
and blessed be the Creator
for the miracle of red potato,
for the miracle of green bean,
for the miracle of fawn
        mushrooms,

and blessed be God
for the miracle of earth:
ancestors, grass, bird,
deer and all gone,
wild creatures
whose bodies become
carrots, peas, and wild
flowers, who
give sustenance
to human hands, whose
agile dance of music
nourishes the ear
and soul of the dog
resting under the stove
and the woman working over
the stove and the geese
out the open window
strolling in the backyard.
And blessed be God
for all, all, all.

ALLA RENEE BOZARTH

All life is your own,
All fruits of the earth
Are fruits of your womb,
Your union, your dance.
Lady and Lord,
We thank you for blessings and abundance.
Join with us, Feast with us, Enjoy with us!
Blessed be.

STARHAWK

All that I have comes from my Mother!
I give myself over to this pot.
My thoughts are on the good, the healing properties of this food.
My hands are balanced, I season well!

I give myself over to this pot.
Life is being given to me.

I commit to sharing, I feed others.
I feed She Who Feeds Me.

I give myself over to this gift.
I adorn this table with food.
I invite lovers and friends to come share.
I thank you for this gift.
All that I have comes from my Mother!

LUISAH TEISH

GATHAS

Holy persons draw to themselves all that is earthly.

HILDEGARD OF BINGEN

I entrust myself to earth,
Earth entrusts herself to me.
I entrust myself to Buddha,
Buddha entrusts herself to me.

THICH NHAT HANH

All are nothing but flowers
In a flowering universe.

NAKAGAWA SOEN-ROSHI

Lord make us mindful of the little things that grow and blossom
in these days to make the world beautiful for us.

W. E. B. DU BOIS

Remember, it is forbidden to live in a town
Which has no garden or greenery.

KIDDUSHIN 4:12

May the axe be far away from you;
May the fire be far away from you;
May there be rain without storm;
Lord of Trees, may you be blessed;
Lord of Trees, may I be blessed.

HINDU PRAYER

Be like a tree in pursuit of your cause.
Stand firm, grip hard, thrust upward, bend to
the winds of heaven, and learn tranquility.

DEDICATION TO RICHARD ST. BARBE BAKER,
FATHER OF THE TREES

When you walk across the fields with your mind pure and holy,
then from all the stones, and all growing things, and all animals,
the sparks of their soul come out and cling to you, and then they
are purified and become a holy fire in you.

HASIDIC SAYING

Watching gardeners label their plants
I vow with all beings
to practice the old horticulture
and let the plants identify me.

ROBERT AITKEN

Where I sit is holy,
Holy is the ground.
Forest, mountain, river,
Listen to the sound.
Great Spirit circle
All around me.

ANONYMOUS

This world is the abode of God,
and God truly lives in the world.

GURU ANGAD

From all that dwells below the skies,
Let faith and hope with joy arise;
Let beauty, truth, and good be sung
Through every land, by every tongue.

UNITARIAN PRAYER

I sing to the Mother Gaia.
I sing to the Father Sun.
I sing to the living in the garden where
The Mother and the Father are One.

ANONYMOUS

How lovely are thy holy groves
    God of heaven and earth
My soul longs and faints
    for the circle of thy trees.
My heart and my flesh
    sing with joy to thee
      O God of life.

CHINOOK PSALTER

May all things move and be moved in me
    and know and be known in me
May all creation
    dance for joy within me.

CHINOOK PSALTER

Mosque is the Earth, and as holy it is,
Pray ye the faithful when the time comes,
Care not for the place wherever it be.

ALAMSAEEN

Religion is Revelation:
all the Wonders of all the Planets striking
all your Only Mind.

Guard the Mysteries!
Constantly reveal Them!

LEW WELCH

Just to be is a blessing.
Just to live is holy.

RABBI ABRAHAM HESCHEL

365

May it be delightful my house;
From my head may it be delightful;
To my feet may it be delightful;
Where I lie may it be delightful;
All above me may it be delightful;
All around me may it be delightful.

NAVAJO CHANT

Beloved Lord, Almighty God!
Through the rays of the sun,
Through the waves of the air,
Through the All-pervading Life in space,
Purify and revivify me, and, I pray,
Heal my body, heart, and soul. Amen

HAZRAT INAYAT KHAN

When I rise up
let me rise up joyful
like a bird

When I fall
let me fall without regret
like a leaf

WENDELL BERRY

Earth brings us into life
and nourishes us.
Earth takes us back again.
Birth and death are present in every moment.

THICH NHAT HANH

The things, good Lord, that we pray for, give
us the grace to labour for.

SAINT THOMAS MORE

367

BLESSED BE THE NIGHT

Twilight is a time for sharing—and a time for
remembering—sharing the fragrance of the
cooling earth—the shadows of the gathering
dusk—

Here our two worlds meet and pass—the
frantic sounds of man grow dimmer as the light
recedes—the unhurried rhythm of the other
world swells in volume as the darkness
deepens—

It is not strange that discord has
no place in this great symphony of sound—
it is not strange that a sense
of peace descends upon all living things—
it is not strange that
memories burn more brightly—as the things of
substance lose their line and form in the softness
of the dark—

Twilight is a time for sharing—and a
time for remembering—remembering the things of
beauty wasted by our careless hands—our frequent
disregard of other living things—the many songs
unheard because we would not listen—

Listen tonight with all the
wisdom of your spirit—listen too with
all the compassion of your heart—
lest there come another night—
when there is only silence—

A great
and
total
silence—

WINSTON ABBOTT

At night make me one with the darkness
In the morning make me one with the light.

WENDELL BERRY

369

Lord God, Light unfailing, Creator of all lights
and Sun of this whole world, bless now the
lighting of this evening lamp; a symbol of your
purity and radiance and a token of your
presence and your power. Amen.

LITURGY OF JYOTINIKETAN COMMUNITY

I reverently speak in the presence of the
    Great Parent God:

I give thee grateful thanks
that Thou hast enabled me to live this day,
the whole day,
in obedience to the excellent spirit of Thy ways.

SHINTO EVENING PRAYER

Bless Adonai
who spins day into dusk
With wisdom watch
the dawn gates open;
with understanding let
time and seasons
come and go;
with awe perceive
the stars in lawful orbit.
Morning dawns,
evening darkens;
darkness and light yielding
one to the other,
yet each distinguished
and unique.

Marvel at Life!
Strive to know its ways!
Seek Wisdom and Truth,
the gateways
to Life's mysteries!

Wondrous indeed
is the evening twilight.

RABBI RAMI M. SHAPIRO

Sweet Spirit of Sleep, who brings peace and rest
to weary bodies,
    Empty us of aches and pains,
    for we struggle as seeds through unyielding earth.
Bring to us the timeless nature of your presence—
the endless void of our slumber.
    Make us aware of the work we can do while in your time
    Make us to know our dreaming,
    where past and future are reconciled.
Come let us honor sleep, that knits up
the raveled sleeve of care, the death of each day's life,
sore labor's bath, balm of hurt minds,
great nature's second course,
chief nourisher in life's feast.

CONGREGATION OF ABRAXAS

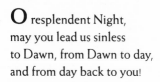

O resplendent Night,
may you lead us sinless
to Dawn, from Dawn to day,
and from day back to you!

ATHARVA VEDA XIX

372

The sun has disappeared,
I have switched off the light,
and my wife and children are asleep.
The animals in the forest are full of fear,
and so are the people on their mats.
They prefer the day with your sun
to the night.
But I still know that your moon is there,
and your eyes and also your hands.
Thus I am not afraid.
This day again
you led us wonder-fully.
Everybody went to his mat
satisfied and full.
Renew us during our sleep,
that in the morning
we may come afresh to our daily jobs.
Be with our brothers far away in Asia
who may be getting up now. Amen.

GHANAIAN CHRISTIAN PRAYER

Goodnight God
I hope that you are having
a good time being the world.
I like the world very much.
I'm glad you made the plants
and trees survive with the
rain and summers.
When summer is nearly near
the leaves begin to fall.
I hope you have a good time
being the world.
I like how God feels around
everyone in the world.
God, I am very happy that
I live on you.
Your arms clasp around the world.
I like you and your friends.
Every time I open my eyes
I see the gleaming sun.
I like the animals—the deer,
and us creatures of the world,
the mammals.
I love my dear friends.

DANU BAXTER,
FOUR AND A HALF YEARS OLD

And now I wish to pray and perform
a ritual of my devotion to the sun.
I will bow and sing beneath my breath,
then perform the dance of farewell
and my confidence in the sun's return.

All is dance; the sun glides along the horizon;
now the leaves sway;
now the earth spins.

DAVID IGNATOW

XI

MEDITATIONS

Meditation has been

described as a journey—a journey from the surface mind to the undifferentiated mind—a journey made by progressively extending calmness and awareness to more and more subtle levels.

Most spiritual traditions have a vast repertoire of contemplative techniques which are used to cultivate this enlightened state. For example, in the Catholic church, prayers of quiet and recollection are used to help still the mind and enhance awareness. In Hinduism and Buddhism breathing techniques, chanting, and visualization are some of the practices used to bring about physical and mental calmness while at the same time heightening our sensitivity and clarity. In all traditions tranquility alone is not the goal. While relaxation may be one of the positive byproducts of the meditative state the goal is rather the systematic development of a non–self-centered perspective.

> As I go into the Earth, she pierces my heart. As I penetrate further, she unveils me. When I have reached her center, I am weeping openly. I have known her all my life, yet she reveals stories to me, and these stories are revelations and I am transformed. . . .[1]

The meditative experience leads to a moment of insight into the process of identification. At that moment, awareness penetrates into the normally unconscious chain of mental events, the chain that gives us the illusion of rock-solid convictions such as "I am so-and-so" and "this really matters." The insight of meditation brings with it a radical and permanent change in this perspective.

The prayers in this section evidence this radical shift. They invite us to leave behind our particular identity—to enter deeply into awareness of the Earth as our sacred reality. If we want to understand something, we cannot just stand outside and observe it. We have to penetrate it, be one with it, in order to really understand it.

As we keenly observe the Earth and its processes, alterations in our perceptions begin to occur; events seem to slow down. Each component of the event seems to contain vast unhurried expanses of time and space. In this silent emptiness the distance separating the starting point and the goal disappears. We recognize our complete identification with the Earth and, indeed, with all that is. If meditation is a journey, it is a journey to where we are. T. S. Eliot captures this experience at the end of his poem "Little Gidding":

*We shall not cease from exploration
and the end of all our exploring
shall be to arrive where we started
and know the place for the first time.*

---
[1] Susan Griffin

As I go into the Earth, she pierces my heart. As I penetrate further, she unveils me. When I have reached her center, I am weeping openly. I have known her all my life, yet she reveals stories to me, and these stories are revelations and I am transformed. Each time I go to her I am born like this. Her renewal washes over me endlessly, her wounds caress me; I become aware of all that has come between us, of the noise between us, the blindness, of something sleeping between us. Now my body reaches out to her. They speak effortlessly, and I learn at no instant does she fail me in her presence. She is as delicate as I am; I know her sentience; I feel her pain and my own pain comes into me, and my own pain grows large and I grasp this pain with my hands, and I open my mouth to this pain, I taste, I know, and I know why shes goes on, under great weight, with this great thirst, in drought, in starvation, with intelligence in every act does she survive disaster. This earth is my sister; I love her daily grace, her silent daring, and how loved I am how we admire this strength in each other, all that we have lost, all that we have suffered, all that we know: we are stunned by this beauty, and I do not forget what she is to me, what I am to her.

SUSAN GRIFFIN

As we are together, praying for peace, let us be truly with each other.

Let us pay attention to our breathing.

Let us be relaxed in our bodies and our minds.

Let us be at peace with our bodies and our minds.

Let us return to ourselves and become wholly ourselves. Let us maintain a half-smile on our faces.

Let us be aware of the source of being common to us all and to all living things.

Evoking the presence of the Great Compassion, let us fill our hearts with our own compassion—towards ourselves and towards all living beings.

Let us pray that all living beings realize that they are all brothers and sisters, all nourished from the same source of life.

Let us pray that we ourselves cease to be the cause of suffering to each other.

Let us plead with ourselves to live in a way which will not deprive other beings of air, water, food, shelter, or the chance to live.

With humility, with awareness of the existence of life, and of the sufferings that are going on around us, let us pray for the establishment of peace in our hearts and on earth. Amen

THICH NHAT HANH

May our corner of the earth join us
in blessing the Lord
fruit-laden papayas, fig-trees in bud . . .
You, guavas, replete with promise,
bougainvillaeas of every colour,
beans that twist and clamber,
tomatoes and all green vegetables,
and you, fields of rice in the valleys,
O praise the marvels of the Lord!

And you, Bamboo, who own neither flower
nor fruits, sing a song of praise to the Lord,
for you are rich in other ways:
supple and lively, hold your head high,
yield before the storm, but do not break.
Your shoots, hugging to one another all close,
will confront the hurricane.
Then, when it's passed,
lift up your head!
And if the typhoon sweeps you away,
let it carry you with it.
Someone will find you lying on the road

or maybe you will kindle a poor man's fire
or be made into a balance-pole
to ease men's burdens!

If need should arise, let yourself be split
into strips by the hand of a clever craftsman.
Thus you will become a mat or a basket,
a broom or a brush—again, on demand,
let yourself be used whole, without hesitation,
to support the sail of a sturdy junk
or enable a fisherman to cast his net.

In you, Bamboo, some will seek inspiration
to guide their brush towards lines of beauty,
or make of you a flute or a pipe.
Let yourself be emptied of self that you may
    sing a melody new.
Some may try to make of you a barrier
to separate people one from another
Then let your leafage vibrate with the rustle
of a call which will resound near and far
and invite them to live in unity and love!

TRANSLATED FROM THE FRENCH BY MARY ROGERS

At start of spring I open a trench
in the ground. I put into it
the winter's accumulation of paper,
pages I do not want to read
again, useless words, fragments,
errors. And I put into it
the contents of the outhouse:
light of the sun, growth of the ground,
finished with one of their journeys.
To the sky, to the wind, then,
and to the faithful trees, I confess
my sins: that I have not been happy
enough, considering my good luck;
have listened to too much noise;
have been inattentive to wonders;
have lusted after praise.
And then upon the gathered refuse
of mind and body, I close the trench,
folding shut again the dark,
the deathless earth. Beneath that seal
the old escapes into the new.

WENDELL BERRY

My friend from Asia has powers and magic, he
      plucks a blue leaf from the young blue-gum
And gazing upon it, gathering and quieting
The God in his mind, creates an ocean more real
      than the ocean, the salt, the actual
Apalling presence, the power of the waters.
He believes that nothing is real except as we make
      it. I humbler have found in my blood
Bred west of Caucasus a harder mysticism.
Multitude stands in my mind but I think that the
      ocean in the bone vault is only
The bone vault's ocean: out there is the ocean's;
The water is the water, the cliff is the rock, come
      shocks and flashes of reality. The mind
Passes, the eye closes, the spirit is a passage;
The beauty of things was born before eyes and
      sufficient to itself; the heart-breaking beauty
Will remain when there is no heart to break for it.

ROBINSON JEFFERS

You sit down on a hill top, or anywhere high enough for you
　　to see nothing, but the sky, in front of your eyes.
With your mind you make everything empty.

There's nothing there, you say.
And you see it like that—nothing
　　　　emptiness.
　　　　　　　Then you say, AH,
　　　　　　but there IS something.
Look, there's the sea,
　　　　and the MOON has risen—
full, round, white.

And you see it like that—
　　　　　　　　　　Sea, silver in the moon light,
　　　　　with little white, topped waves. And in the
　　　　　Blue Black sky above
hangs a great moon Bright,
　　　　but not dazzling,
a soft brightness you might say.
　　　　You stare at the moon a long,
long time, feeling calm, happy.
　　　　　　then the moon gets *smaller*,
but brighter and brighter and brighter till you see it as a
　　　　　　pearl, or a seed, but so bright
　　　　　you can only *just bear* to look at it. The Pearl

starts to grow. And before you know what's happened it's
KUAN YIN herself, standing up against the sky
all dressed in gleaming white
and with her feet resting on a lotus
that floats in the waves.

You see her
once you know how to do it
as clearly as I see you,
Her Robes
are shining
and there's a halo
round her head.
She smiles at you
such a lovely smile. She's so glad
to see you that tears of happiness sparkle
in her eyes.
If you keep your mind calm,
by just whispering her name
and not trying too hard

she will stay a long
long time
When she does go
it's by getting smaller.
She doesn't go back to being a pearl

But just gets so small
       That at last you can't see her. Then you notice
that the sky and sea
have vanished too.
       Just Space is left.
Lovely, Lovely, Space, going on forever.
       That Space stays long
if you can do without *you*. Not you *and* space, you see
       Just Space.
       No you.

CANTONESE WOMAN

Step out onto the Planet.
Draw a circle a hundred feet round.

Inside the circle are
300 things nobody understands, and, maybe
nobody's ever really seen.

How many can you find?

LEW WELCH

389

Within a circle of one meter
You sit, pray and sing.

Within a shelter ten meters large
You sleep well, rain sounds a lullaby.

Within a field a hundred meters large
Raise rice and goats.

Within a valley a thousand meters large
Gather firewood, water, wild vegetables, and Amanitas.

Within a forest ten kilometers large
Play with raccoons, hawks,
Poison snakes and butterflies.

Mountainous country Shinano
A hundred kilometers large
Where someone lives leisurely, they say.

Within a circle ten thousand kilometers large
Go to see the southern coral reef in summer
Or winter drifting ices in the sea of Okhotsk.

Within a circle ten thousand kilometers large
Walking somewhere on the earth.

Within a circle a hundred thousand kilometers large
Swimming in the sea of shooting stars.

Within a circle a million kilometers large
Upon the spaced-out yellow mustard blossoms
The moon in the east, the sun west.

Within a circle ten billion kilometers large
Pop far out of the solar system mandala.

Within a circle ten thousand light years large
The Galaxy full blooming in spring.

Within a circle one billion light years large
Andromeda is melting away into snowing cherry flowers.

Now within a circle ten billion light years large
All thoughts of time, space are burnt away
There again you sit, pray and sing
You sit, pray and sing.

NANAO SAKAKI

At the center of the earth there is a mother.
If any of us who are her children choose to die
she feels a grief like a wound deeper
than any of us can imagine.
She puts her hands to her face
like this: her palms open.
Put them there like she does.
Her fingers press into her eyes.
Do that, too.
She tries to howl.
Some of us have decided
this mother cannot hear all of us
in our desperate wishes.
Here, in this time,
our hearts have been cut into small chambers
like ration cards
and we can no longer imagine every
morsel nor each tiny
thought at once,
as she still can.

This is normal,
she tries to tell us,
but we don't listen.
Sometimes someone has a faint memory
of all this, and
she suffers.
She is wrong to imagine
she suffers alone.
Do you think we are not all hearing and speaking
at the same time?
Our mother is somber.
She is thinking.
She puts her big ear
against the sky
to comfort herself.
Do this. She calls to us,
Do this.

SUSAN GRIFFIN

And now we will count to twelve
and we will all keep still . . .

For once on the face of the earth
let's not speak in any language;
let's stop for one second,
and not move our arms so much.

It would be an exotic moment
without rush, without engines,
we would all be together
in a sudden strangeness.

Fishermen in the cold sea
would not harm whales
and the man gathering salt
would look at his hurt hands.

Those who prepare green wars,
wars with gas, wars with fire,
victory with no survivors,
would put on clean clothes
and walk about with their brothers
in the shade, doing nothing.

What I want should not be confused
with total inactivity.
(Life is what it is about;
I want no truck with death.)

If we were not so singleminded
about keeping our lives moving,
and for once could do nothing,
perhaps a huge silence
might interrupt this sadness
of never understanding ourselves
and of threatening ourselves with death.

Perhaps the earth can teach us
as when everything seems dead
and later proves to be alive.

Now I'll count up to twelve,
and you keep quiet and I will go.

PABLO NERUDA

Grasshopper, your tiny song
And my poem alike belong
To the dark and silent earth,
From which all poetry has birth;
All we say and all we sing
Is but as the murmuring
Of that drowsy heart of hers
When from her deep dream she stirs:
If we sorrow, or rejoice
You and I are but her voice.

Deftly does the dust express,
In mind, her hidden loveliness—
And, from her cool silence, stream
The cricket's cry and Dante's dream;
For the earth, that breeds the trees,
Breeds cities too, and symphonies,
Equally her beauty flows
Into a savior, or a rose—
Looks down in dream, and from above
Smiles at herself in Jesus' love;
Christ's love and Homer's art
Are but the working of her heart
Through Leonardo's hand she seeks
Herself, and through Beethoven speaks

In holy thunderings that sound
The awful message of the ground.

The serene and humble mold
Does in herself all selves enfold,
Kingdoms, destinies, and creeds,
Proud dreams, heroic deeds,
Science, that probes the firmament,
The high, inflexible intent
Of one, for many, sacrificed;
Plato's brain, the heart of Christ,
All love, all legend, and all lore
Are in the dust forevermore.

Even as the growing grass,
Up from the soil religions pass,
And the field that bears the rye
Bears parables and prophecy—
Out of the earth the poem grows,
Like the lily, or the rose;
And all man is, or yet may be,
Is but herself in agony
Toiling up the steep ascent
Toward the complete accomplishment
When all dust shall be—the whole
Universe—one conscious soul.

Ah, the quiet and cool sod
Bears in her breast the dream of God.

If you would know what earth is, scan
The intricate, proud heart of man,
Which is the earth articulate,
And learn how holy and how great,
How limitless, and how profound,
Is the nature of the ground—
How, without question or demur,
We may entrust ourselves to her
When we are wearied out and lay
Our bodies in the common clay.

For she is pity, she is love,
All wisdom, she, all thoughts that move
About her everlasting breast
Till she gathers them to rest—
All tenderness of all the ages,
Seraphic secrets of the sages,
Vision and hope of all the seers,
All prayer, all anguish, and all tears,
Are but the dust, that from her dream
Awakes, and knows herself supreme;
Are but earth, when she reveals
All that her secret heart conceals

Down in the dark and silent loam,
Which is ourselves, asleep, at home,.

Yes, and this, my poem, too,
Is part of her as dust and dew—
Wherein herself she doth declare,
Through my lips, and say her prayer.

JOHN HALL WHEELOCK

399

A CALENDAR OF
EARTH PRAYERS

FOR TENS OF THOUSANDS
of years our ancestors set aside special days to mark their spiritual participation in the great cycles of life. These days of prayer and ritual were timed to coincide with the changing relations of Earth, sun, and stars throughout the year. Solstices and equinoxes are among the oldest of Earth holidays, marking the points of extreme and balance between darkness and light. Later, cross-quarter days (halfway between the solstices and equinoxes) were used to denote additional seasonal change points in the yearly round. Among the Celts, for example, the feast of Beltane, or May Day as we now know it, marks the halfway point between the Vernal Equinox and the Summer Solstice and expresses the coming-into-being of the

equinox's promise. It also balances Samhain, or Halloween, occurring half a year later. These solar-earth cycles determine the dates of most of our seasonal celebrations, religious and secular, and remind us again that the earthly and the spiritual share a common rhythm.

In pre-agricultural times, animal life was an important point of connection with the Earth. Specific dates were celebrated to mark the return of animal herds to their winter and summer quarters. With the gradual development of sedentary agriculture, women and men became more conscious of the life-giving cycles of plants. The cycles of growth, fruition, harvest, and rest still drive our calendar, and many Jewish and Christian holidays trace their roots to these early agricultural origins. In every historical time and culture these days of Earth celebration served as ways of strengthening community life by observing our common participation in the rhythms of the natural world.

On the following pages we suggest a way of using this collection of Earth Prayers on special days to renew our sense of commonality with the Earth and all its creatures. We start with the seasonal calendar, adding holidays from different religious and cultural traditions. We also have taken the liberty of suggesting Earth-related remembrances in harmony with the spirit of various holy days. Yet this calendar of Earth Prayers does not attempt to give a complete Earth liturgy, since any true Earth liturgical calendar must be rooted in a specific place or region. In that regard we also note the unavoidable bias we have toward the Northern Hemisphere. Our hope is that this calendar can serve as a basis for creating a personal Earth liturgy specific to the seasonal events of your region.

If you are interested in developing your own local Earth calendar, you will want to find out about the natural and cultural history of the area in which you live. What are the migration patterns and rhythms of different animals and birds? When do the salmon begin their run upstream? When do the song birds return to your home? What days did the native peoples of your region celebrate? What about other ethnic groups that settled in your area—what are their feasts and holidays? When are the birthdays of local environmentalists—women and men who made a mark in helping to preserve the vitality and beauty of your region? Dates such as these can be integrated with the more general holidays suggested here.

Through the daily practice of Earth Prayer we can renew our sense of reverence for the natural world. We can discover in ourselves the sacred truth that all things are interconnected. And we can be moved to do everything in our power to help bring back clean water, fresh air, abundant trees, and fruitful soil.

Numbers following each entry refer to page numbers on which specific prayers can be found. The letters "a," "b," or "c" direct the reader to the first, second, or third prayer on the page.

JANUARY

1   New Year's Day—Celebration of Peace with all Creation (94)

3   Death of Joy Adamson in Kenya, 1980—Author of *Born Free* and defender of wildlife (250a)

4   Earth Perihelion—Day the Earth is closest to the sun (140)

5   National Bird Day (256)

6   Epiphany—Celebration of the creativity of the dark (327)

14 Birthday of Albert Schweitzer—Humanitarian and friend of animals (254a)

16 Martin Luther King, Jr. Day—Extending the universal human struggle for freedom and justice to all creatures (110)

17 Yearly migration of gray whales along the western North American coast (278)

19 Greek Epiphany—Blessing of the water (143)

22 Anniversary of the surrender of his native lands by Chief Seatlh (Seattle) to the President of the United States, 1854 (10)

JANUARY

Movable days:

> World Religions' Day—Worldwide day of meditation and prayer for the Earth (228)
>
> Tu B'shivat—Jewish celebration of the Trees (54)
>
> Makara Sankranti—Indian festival celebrating the passing of the Winter Solstice (329a)
>
> Iroquois Midwinter Ceremony—A day to invoke healing for the tribe (96)
>
> Plow Monday (first Monday after Epiphany)—Blessing of tools, plows, and other work implements in preparation for Spring planting (305)
>
> Full Moon Day—The Wolf Moon, time to remember the hungry and homeless of the Earth (83)

FEBRUARY

1   Feast of St. Brigit—Derived from festival of Brigid, the Celtic goddess of maidens, evoking the movement of life from winter to springtime (297)

2   Imbolic or Candlemas Day—Cross-quarter day (halfway between winter solstice and spring equinox), marks the return of the light and the transformation within us from an inner contemplative focus toward outer manifestation (181b)

4   Birthday of Charles Lindbergh (1902–1974)—Commemorating the allure of the sky (148a)

10   Lantern Festival—Chinese Festival of Lights (194)

12   Festival of Diana (Artemis)—Ancient goddess protector of wildlife and forest (281)

14   Valentine's Day (289)

15   Lupercalia—Ancient Roman festival honoring the heat or sexual readiness that permeates all nature (292); Birthday of Galileo Galilei (1564–1642)—Feast of the Planets (216)

16   Nirvana Day—Observes passing of Sakyamuni into Enlightenment (24)

19   Presidents' Day—Day to acknowledge importance of leadership for a healthy planet (110)

FEBRUARY

23 Anniversary of Supernova 1987—Festival of the Exploding Stars (198)

29 Leap Year Day—A day to consider the passing of time and the joy of the unexpected (208)

Movable days:

Baika-Sai—Japanese plum-blossom festival, a time for appreciating flowering trees (295b)

Mardi Gras—Carnival Season around the world, rejoicing in the return of the light (338)

Shambala Day—Tibetan New Year (381)

Shivaratri—Hindu Festival devoted to Shiva, the powerful God of destruction and renewal (23)

Shrove Tuesday—Traditional day for clearing luxuries out of the house in preparation for Lenten fasting (92)

Tet Nguyen Dan and Chinese New Year—Lunar New Year celebrated in Vietnam, China, and Korea (93)

Full Moon Day—The Snow Moon (197)

MARCH

1   Anniversary of establishment of Yellowstone National Park, 1872—Commitment to preservation of wild lands (80)

8   International Women's Day—Celebration of the feminine within nature (14)

9   Ancient Roman festival of Aphrodite and Adonis—Celebration of love and fertility (4)

11 Johnny Appleseed Day—Patron of orchards in the United States (44b)

12 Crane Watch Day—Nebraska celebrates arrival of Sandhill cranes along Platte River (251b)

14 Birthday of Albert Einstein—Father of contemporary physics (390)

16 Curlew Day—Traditional arrival of long-billed curlews in Oregon (256)

17 St. Patrick's Day (190)

19 National Agriculture Day—The swallows return to San Juan Capistrano for the summer (221)

21 Vernal Equinox—Marks the beginning of spring and the point of equal balance between light and dark (293b)

24 Maple Syrup festival in Vermont—Festival welcoming spring and the greening of the Earth (296a)

MARCH

25 Feast of the Annunciation—Day on which the Equinox is over, day is now longer than night, and light has conquered darkness (195b)

Movable days:

World Day of Prayer—Ecumenical event reinforcing the bonds between peoples of different cultures (96)

Purim—Esther petitions the king to free the Jews; we petition our leaders for a free and healthy planet (113)

Ramadan—Begins Muslim month of holy days of purification and fasting (56)

Ash Wednesday—Day after Shrove Tuesday. Begins Lent, a forty-day period of Christian penance and fasting in spiritual preparation for the rebirth of Easter (384)

Magna Puja—Buddhist celebration of spiritual community (11)

Laetare Sunday and Mothering Sunday (fourth Sunday of Lent)—Celebration of sprouting trees and grains, ancient festival dedicated to Mother Earth (46)

Holi—Hindu celebration of the advent of spring season (52)

Full Moon Day—The Worm Moon, day of prayers for preparation of the soil (304b)

APRIL

3   Ram Navami—Hindu celebration of the god Rama (385)

5   Buddhist Feast of Kuan Yin/Avalokitashavara—Recognizing our capacity for compassion with all creation (266a)

6   North Pole Day—Celebration of Arctic and Antarctic wilderness (81)

7   World Health Day (116)

8   Celebration of Buddha's Birthday in the Zen tradition (120)

13   Ancient Roman festival of Ceres—Day of prayer for the coming agricultural season (305)

14   National Dolphin Day—Remembrance of all sea creatures (278)

21   Birthday of John Muir (1838–1914)—Advocate of forest and wilderness conservation (154c)

22   International Earth Day—First observed April 22, 1970 (394)

26   Birthday of John James Audubon, ornithologist and artist—Celebration of the birds (259)

27   Teej—Hindu holiday celebrating the arrival of annual monsoon rains (150)

APRIL

Movable days:

Battle of the Flowers—Ancient Aztec spring festival (302)

Passover or Pesach—Jewish feast of unleavened bread and festival of freedom (47)

Palm Sunday—How easily we join a crowd to shout fashionable slogans of the day and forget our responsibilities a day later (93)

Good Friday—A time to recognize the similarities between Christ's passion and the passion of the Earth (185)

Easter—First Sunday after full moon following vernal equinox: celebration of the Resurrection of Jesus and the rebirth of nature from its winter sleep (294)

National Arbor Day (last Friday in April)—A day to acknowledge the beauty and gifts of trees (55)

Cherry Blossom Festival—A time to appreciate the briefness of the spring season (303)

Kalpa Vruksha—Spring festival in India, occasion of tree planting (304b)

Full Moon Day—The Pink Moon, time when Earth is in the pink of health and vitality (175)

411

MAY

1 Beltane—May Day festival, cross-quarter day (halfway between Spring equinox and Summer solstice); celebrated for thousands of years as the point of fertility and beauty of the flowering Earth (307)

2 Fire Festival—Ancient Roman holiday of the Sun (196)

3 Sun Day—Proclaimed by Carter administration to focus attention on potential of solar energy (140)

5 Cinco de Mayo (133b)

6 Shepherds' and Herdsmen's Day—Old folk festival in Eastern Europe to celebrate returning the animals to pasture (251a)

18 Festival of Pan—Greek celebration of all that is male in the universe (206)

19 Well-Dressing Day—Ancient English day for dressing wells with flowers to give thanks for the water provided (143)

25 Africa Freedom Day (202)

30 Birth of Buddha celebrated in the Tibetan tradition (49)

31 Visitation of the Blessed Virgin Mary—A time to help with the greening of the Earth (98)

MAY

Movable days:

Be Kind to Animals Week—First week in May (270)

Memorial Day—Day of remembrance of the costs of war (173b)

Wesak—The birth, enlightenment, and paranirvana of the Buddha celebrated at the full moon of May (44a)

Ascension—Forty days after Easter; a time to celebrate the clouds and the cycles of moisture as it is drawn up into the sky and then falls again as nourishing rain (326)

Festival of Whitsun, or Pentecost—Fifty days after Easter; ancient feast of first fruits as they ripen under the powerful influence of the sun (232)

Shavuot—Fifty days after Passover; celebration of giving of the Torah at Mt. Sinai and ancient Jewish harvest festival (112)

Rain Dance Festival in Guatemala—Prayers for a fruitful summer season (152)

International Mother's Day—Commemoration of Mother Earth and all the mothers of the Earth (205)

Full Moon Day—The Full Flower Moon or the Corn Planting Moon (302)

JUNE

2 Seamen's Day—Celebrated in Iceland to protect the fishermen during the summer (21)

4 Rosalia Day—Ancient festival of roses (223)

5 World Environment Day—Established by the United Nations, 1972, to reaffirm worldwide need for care for the environment (118)

13 Children's Day in the United States (32)

17 Marriage of Orpheus and Eurydice in Greek mythology—Celebration of married love; commitment and bonding after the sexual excitement of May (286)

22 Summer Solstice—Strongest solar energy of the year; festival to honor the power of the Sun (339)

23 Midsummer's Eve—Festival to receive the light and remember to use well all that we have received (240)

24 Feast of St. John the Baptist, Midsummer Day—Welcome of summer (236)

24 Inti Raymi—Ancient Inca Festival of the Sun (159)

JUNE

Movable days:

>Father's Day—Celebration of masculine stewardship within the Earth community (122)

>Children's festivals around the world—Blessing all that is young (301)

>Rath Yatra—Hindu festival to the Lord of the universe (241)

>Hajj—Islamic holy day marking the first day of pilgrimage to Mecca (334b)

>Environmental Sabbath—Sunday nearest World Environment Day (82)

>Full Moon Day—Strawberry Moon or Rose Moon (182)

JULY

3   Green Corn Dance—Seminole Indian festival giving thanks for first harvest (309)

4   United States Independence Day—Celebration of our interdependence with all living beings (43)

5   Earth Aphelion—Day Earth is farthest from the sun; also anniversary of supernova that created the Crab Nebula in 1054 (224)

7   Dhamma Day—Celebrates the Buddha's first teaching and begins a period of prayer and sacrifice during the rains (242)

13   Feast of our Lady of Fatima in Portugal and ancient Greek Festival of Demeter—A day of prayer for healing of the Earth (109)

14   French Bastille Day—A day to consider the liberty and kinship of all creation (174)

15   Obon—Japanese Lantern festival that honors departed ancestors (321)

17   Festival of Amaterasu-o-Mi-Kami—Japanese festival of the female Sun goddess (162)

20   Moon Day—Commemorates historic landing of humans on the moon, 1969 (386)

JULY

Movable days:

> Hurricane Supplication Day—Fourth Monday in July in Virgin Islands; a day of prayer for safety through stormy seasons (186)

> Native American Sundance Festival (192)

> Muslim New Year (94)

> Bon—Buddhist occasion for rejoicing in the enlightenment offered by the Buddha, referred to as "Gathering of Joy" (108)

> Asalha Puja (Buddhist) and Guru Purnima (Hindu)—Celebrated on the full moon, time to honor our spiritual teachers and the revelation of the Earth (188)

> Full Moon Day—The Thunder Moon; remember importance of rain for this season's crops (151)

AUGUST

1   Lammas—Cross-quarter day (halfway between summer solstice and autumn equinox); festival of new bread, forerunner of autumn harvest festivals. Signifies withdrawal of energy into the Earth in preparation for the falling seeds that are to germinate in winter (312)

6   Hiroshima Day—Anniversary of dropping of first atomic bomb on Japan, 1945 (84a)

7   Anniversary of first photograph of Earth from space (6)

11   Feast of St. Claire—Time to remember the joys of living a simple life (109)

12   Persiod Meteor Showers (216)

15   Assumption of the Blessed Virgin Mary—August gardens overflow with abundance; festival of Mary's passover and harvesting into heaven (309)

26   Krakatoa Day—Anniversary of volcanic eruption, 1883, that affected the atmosphere and the oceans for years (200)

AUGUST

Movable days:

> Choosuk or Moon Festivals—Observed in Korea at end of harvest (311)
>
> Onam—Hindu harvest festival (318)
>
> Janmashtami—Hindu celebration commemorating birth of Lord Krishna (173b)
>
> Hopi Snake Dance Festival—Praying to Great Spirit for rain (149a)
>
> Full Moon Day—The Red Moon (167)

SEPTEMBER

8 "Down driving" begins—In preagricultural times this marked the beginning of the return of animal herds to their winter pastures; later the date became the feast of the nativity of the Blessed Virgin Mary (252)

15 Feast of Holy Cross and Feast of Our Lady of Sorrows—A day for mourning the extinction of species (268)

16 United Nations International Day of Peace (179)

22 Autumnal Equinox—Marks the beginning of the autumn harvest season; as with the vernal equinox the light and dark are in balance (314)

23 Worldwide Day of Prayer and Meditation to Help Heal Mother Earth—First announced in 1990 by "Fellowship of Prayer" (95)

29 Michaelmas Day—A day of courage and hope as we defend the Earth (319a)

SEPTEMBER

Movable days:

Chinese Harvest Festival (358)

Labor Day—Celebration of the end of summer (313)

Jewish month of Ellul—Time of renewal and reconciliation with the natural world (92)

Rosh Hashanah—Jewish new year, birthday of the world (57)

Yom Kippur—Jewish day of atonement (380)

Full Moon Day—The Harvest Moon (315b)

OCTOBER

2 Birthday of Mahatma Gandhi—Reminder to live simply (108)

4 Feast of St. Francis of Assisi—Patron saint of ecology; good day for blessing animals and pets (226)

8 Columbus Day—Day of remembrance and celebration of Native American teachings about the Earth (15)

10 Canadian Day of Thanksgiving (351)

16 World Food Day—Sponsored by the United Nations (347a)

23 The swallows leave San Juan Capistrano Mission in California and head for their winter home (316)

24 United Nations Day—Day of global concern for the Earth (82)

31 Samhain, All Hallows' Eve, Halloween—Cross-quarter day (halfway between autumn equinox and winter solstice): the seed now begins its time of gestation, the harvest is gathered, the fields lie fallow, and the gates of life and death are open (321)

OCTOBER

Movable days:

Sukkot—Eight-day Jewish feast of tabernacles, ancient seasonal celebration of gathering of summer crops (358)

Simchat Torah (last day of Sukkat)—Time to cycle back to beginning of the Torah and reinforce our commitment to recycling all that we use (112)

Durga Puja—Indian festival of the Divine Mother celebrating the creative feminine force within the universe (46)

Han Lu ("the dew grows cold")—Chinese festival marking the end of summer (315b)

International Rainforest Week (second or third week of October) (80)

Peace with Justice Week (207)

Full Moon Day—The Hunter's Moon (261)

NOVEMBER

1   All Saints' Day—A day of thanks and remembrance for all the creatures that give their lives that we may live (264)

2   All Souls' Day—Feast of the Dead (29)

5   World Community Day—Sponsored by Church Women United (28)

9   Berlin Wall came down, 1989 (173b)

11   Martinmas—Final harvest festival (306)

12   Anniversary of great dust storms of 1934 in the American Midwest, which swept away millions of tons of top soil (287)

15   International Fast for a World Harvest—Sponsored by Oxfam (351)

NOVEMBER

Movable days:

Thanksgiving Day—Fourth Thursday in November, a day to honor Native Americans and offer thanks for the abundance and nourishment of the Earth (236)

Diwali—Indian New Year and Hindu festival of triumph of light over darkness and good over evil (370a)

Pavarana—Celebrates Buddha's return to the Earth after spending one season preaching in Heaven (220)

Full Moon Day—The Beaver Moon, time of preparation for winter and reminder to recreate ourselves (325)

DECEMBER

3   Bhopal poison gas disaster, 1984 (69b)

7   Feast of St. Ambrose—Patron Saint of domestic animals (266b)

8   Feast of the Immaculate Conception—Celebration of the Incarnation of Spirit, a time of deep receptivity (344a)

10 International Human Rights Day—A day to reflect on the rights of all peoples (124)

12 Feast of Our Lady of Guadalupe (98)

13 St. Lucia's Day—Ancient Swedish feast of lights (342)

21 Winter Solstice—Ancient holiday marking the longest night of the year (324a)

22 International Arbor Day—A day devoted to encouraging winter tree planting (54)

25 Christmas Day—Birthday of Jesus, beginning of twelve days of Christian celebration of the coming of the Divine Light to the world (172)

31 New Year's Eve—A time of reflection and renewal (286)

DECEMBER

Movable days:

> Advent Season—Four weeks of Christian spiritual preparation for the coming of the light; one possibility is weekly prayers on each of the four elements (204)

> Hanukkah—Eight-day Jewish festival of the lights set at the dark of the moon, an opportunity to reaffirm one's spiritual dedication to Earth work in the coming year (371)

> Bodhi Day, Rohatsu—Celebration of the Buddha's enlightenment according to the Zen tradition (49)

> Ta Chin—Taoist festival of reflection and renewal (228)

> Full Moon Day—The Cold Moon (178a)

INDEX OF FIRST LINES

429

430

432

438

ACKNOWLEDGMENTS

Grateful acknowledgment is made to the following for permission to reprint material copyrighted or controlled by them:

Antler for "The Dark Inside a Life" and "After All Is Said And Done" © 1986. Reprinted by permission of the author.

"Wild Geese," from the book *Dream Work* by Mary Oliver, © 1986 used by permission of the Atlantic Monthly Press.

Baha'i Prayers, © 1954, © 1982, 1985 National Spiritual Assembly of the Baha'is of the United States.

Excerpt from *The Sacred Hoop*, by Paula Gunn Allen, © 1986 by Paula Gunn Allen. Reprinted by permission of Beacon Press.

Permission to quote from *Meditations with Meister Eckhart*, introduction and versions by Matthew Fox, OP, © 1983 by Bear & Company, Inc.; from *Meditations of Bingen*, versions and introduction by Gabriele Uhlein, OSF, © 1983 by Bear & Company, Inc.; from *Meditations with Julian of Norwich*, introduction & versions by Brendan Doyle, © 1983 by Bear & Company, Inc.; and "Prayer of the Seven Galactic Directions," from *Surfers of the Zuvuya* by José Argüelles, © 1988 by José Argüelles, has been granted by the publisher, Bear & Company, PO Drawer 2860, Santa Fe, NM 87504-2860.

Draco Foundation, The Bear Tribe, for Mary Austin's "Charm for Going Hunting" and "Morning Prayer" from *Snowy Earth Comes Gliding*, edited by Evelyn Easton, 1974. Reprinted by permission of the publisher.

Daniel Berrigan, © 1978, "A Mercy, A Healing, Psalm 64," and "Glory Glory Psalm 19." Reprinted by permission of the author.

Bilingual Press/Editorial Bilingüe, Arizona State University, Tempe, Arizona for excerpts from *Poems of the Aztec People*, translated and introduced by Edward Kissam and Michael Schmidt, 1983. Reprinted by permission of the publisher.

Bernice P. Bishop Museum Press, for excerpts from *Hawaiian Antiquities* by David Malo. Reprinted by permission of Bernice P. Bishop Museum Press, Honolulu, Hawaii.

Black Sparrow Press, for "Songs of the Teton Sioux," adapted by James Koller, from *Poems to the Blue Sky*, 1976. Reprinted by permission of Black Sparrow Press, 24 Tenth St., Santa Rosa, CA 95401.

Blackberry Books for "The Bear Trees" from *Talking in Your Sleep* by Kate Barnes, 1986; and for excerpts from *First Sight of Land* by Gary Lawless, 1990. Reprinted by permission of publisher and authors. Blackberry Books, RR 1, Box 228, Nobleboro, ME, 04555.

Robert Bly, © 1980 for translations of Hermann Hesse's "Sometimes," and Zuni Prayer, from *News from the Universe: Poems of Twofold Consciousness*, Sierra Club Books, San Francisco. Reprinted with permission of the author.

Alla Renee Bozarth for "Belonging," from *Stars in Your Bones*, North Star Press, 1990; for "Bakerwoman God," in *Woman Priest: A Personal Odyssey*, Paulist Press, 1988; for "Blessing of the Stewpot," Wisdom House, Sandy, OR. Reprinted by permission of the author.

"The Practice of Loving Kindness," texts compiled and translated by Nanamoli Thera (Wheel No. 7), Kandy, Sri Lanka, Buddhist Publication Society, 1958. Reprinted by permission of the publisher.

"The Day We Die," from *The Rebirth of the Ostrich*, translated by Arthur Markowitz, Campbell Museum, Gaborone, Botswana, 1971.

The Estate of Pablo Neruda, "Keeping Quiet," from *Extravagaria*, translated by Alastair Reed, Jonathan Cape Ltd., London, 1974. Reprinted by permission of the publisher.

Center Publications for "Paying Homage and Acquiring the Essence," as translated by Professor Francis Cook, in *How to Raise an Ox*, Center Publications, Los Angeles, 1978. Reprinted by permission of the publisher.

Cherokee Publications for excerpts from *American Indian Prayers & Poems*, edited by J. Ed Sharpe, 1985. Cherokee Publications, PO Box 256, Cherokee, NC 28719. Reprinted by permission of the publisher.

Church Missionary Society © 1985, "An African Canticle" and "Prayer of a young Ghanaian Christian" from *Morning, Noon, and Night*, edited by Rev. John Carden, 1985. Reprinted by permission of The Church Missionary Society.

"I want to plant a heart in the earth" by Rosario Murillo, from *Volcan: Poems from Central America*, edited by Alejandro Murguía and Barbara Paschke, City Lights Books, San Francisco, 1983. Reprinted by permission of the editors.

Collins Liturgy Publications for excerpts from *Heart of Prayer* by Anthony Gittens, Collins Liturgy Publications, London, 1985. Reprinted by permission of the publisher.

Congregation of Abraxas for excerpts from *The Book of Hours*, © 1985. Reprinted by permission of Congregation of Abraxas, A Unitarian Universalist Order for Liturgical and Spiritual Renewal.

Copper Canyon Press for *Unremembered Country* by Susan Griffin, © 1987. Reprinted by permission of the publisher and author.

Crossroad Publishing Company © 1981 for excerpts from *Praise the Lord in Psalms* by Ernesto Cardenal, translated by Thomas Blackburn. Search Press © 1981. Reprinted by permission of the publishers.

Crown Publishers, *Creativity & Taoism* by Chang Chung-Yuan, 1963. Reprinted by permission of the publisher.

Aivilik Eskimo, "Weather Chant," Thule Eskimo, "Magic Song For Him Who Wishes To Live," Iglulik Eskimo, "Magic Prayer," *I Breathe a New Song: Poems of the Eskimo*, edited by Edmund Carpenter, J.M. Dent & Sons, Toronto, 1959.

Doubleday & Co. for excerpt from *The Sound of the Mountain Water* by Wallace Stegner, copyright © 1969 by Wallace Stegner; excerpts from *When the Earth Was Young: Songs of the American Indian*, edited by David Yeadon. Copyright © 1978 by David Yeadon; "The Abyss" copyright © 1963, "All Morning" copyright © 1964 by Beatrice Roethke, Administratrix of the Estate of Theodore Roethke. From *The Collected Poems of Theodore Roethke*; excerpt from *The Trees Stand Shining* by Hettie Jones, copyright © 1971 by Hettie Jones. All used by permission Doubleday & Co., a division of Bantam Doubleday Dell Publishing Group, Inc.

442

"The Temple of Animals," reprinted with permission of the Literary Estate of Robert Duncan.

From *Appalachian Wilderness: The Great Smoky Mountains* by Eliot Porter and Edward Abbey. Copyright © 1970 by Eliot Porter. Reprinted by permission of the publisher Dutton, an imprint of New American Library, a division of Penguin Books USA, Inc.

Ecco Press for "From March '79," © 1985 by John F. Deane, translator. From *Tomas Transtromer: Selected Poems, 1954–1986*, first published by The Ecco Press in 1987. Reprinted by permission of the publisher.

Faber & Faber, Ltd. for eleven lines from T. S. Eliot's "Ash Wednesday," *Collected Poems 1906–1962*, 1963. Reprinted by permission of Faber & Faber, Ltd.

Reprinted by permission of Harold Ober Associates, Inc. Eleanor Farjean, "Morning has broken." © 1957.

Farrar, Straus & Giroux for "Cover My Earth Mother," "It Was the Wind," "The Day Has Risen," and adaptation of "Prayer" from *In the Trail of the Wind*, edited by John Bierhorst © 1971. Reprinted by permission of Farrar, Straus & Giroux.

Forest of Peace Books for Edward Hays' "Autumn Psalm of Contentment," *Prayers for a Planetary Pilgrim*, 1988. Reprinted by permission of the publisher.

Carole Forman for words to "Antarctica," music by Gene Ashton. © Reprinted with permission of the author.

Graywolf Press for Vicente Huidobro's "Canto I" from *Altazor*, translated by Eliot Weinberger, 1988. Reprinted by permission of the publisher.

Jean Pearson © 1987 from "A Daily Prayer," *On Speaking Terms with Earth*, Great Elm Press, 1988. Reprinted by permission of the author.

The Estate of Lew Welch and Grey Fox Press for excerpts from *Ring of Bone: Collected Poems, 1950–71* by Lew Welch, edited by Donald Allen, 1973. Reprinted by permission of Grey Fox Press, San Francisco, 1973.

Hancock House Publishers Ltd. for "My Heart Soars" by Chief Dan George, from *Saanichtoni*, 1974.

Harcourt Brace Jovanovich, Inc. for "The Peace of Wild Things," *Openings*, © 1968 by Wendell Berry; and for "Glass House Canticle," *The Complete Poems of Carl Sandburg*,

443

©1950 by Carl Sandburg, and renewed © 1978 by Margaret Sandburg, Helga Sandburg Crile, and Janet Sandburg. Reprinted by permission of Harcourt Brace Jovanovich, Inc.

Holt, Rinehart, Winston Publishers, a division of Harcourt Brace Jovanovich for "The Most of It," *The Poetry of Robert Frost,* edited by Edward Connery Lathem, © 1969. Reprinted by permission of Harcourt Brace Jovanovich, Inc.

HarperCollins Publishers for excerpts from *Mother Earth Spirituality: Native American Paths to Healing Ourselves and Our World* by Ed McGaa, © 1990; for excerpt from "Ruhr-Gebiet," in *Collected Poems 1947–1980* by Allen Ginsberg, © 1984 by Allen Ginsberg; for excerpts from *Holy the Firm,* © 1977 by Annie Dillard; for excerpts from *Hymn of the Universe* by Pierre Teilhard de Chardin, © 1969 by Editions du Seuil, English translation © 1965 by William Collins Sons & Co., Ltd., London and Harper & Row, Publishers, Inc.; for excerpts from *The Spiral Dance* by Starhawk, © 1979 by Miriam Simos. "Forest: The Way We Stand," "The Wind," "The Earth: What she is to me," from *Woman & Nature: The Roaring Inside Her,* by Susan Griffin, © 1978 by Susan Griffin. "Kabbalat Shabbat," from *The Book of Blessings: A Feminist-Jewish Reconstruction of Prayer,* by Marcia Falk, © 1990 by Marcia Falk. Poem by Birago Diop and "Blessing While Cooking" from *Jambalaya* by Luisah Teish, © 1985. "August" by Federico Garcia Lorca, translated by James Wright and "Bird's Nest" by Gloria Fuertes, translated by W. S. Merwin, in *Roots and Wings: Poetry from Spain 1900–1975,* edited by Hardie St. Martin, © 1976 by Hardie St. Martin. "How strange and wonderful is our home, our earth," from *Appalachian Wilderness,* by Edward Abbey. Reprinted by permission of HarperCollins Publishers.

Houghton Mifflin for "Song for the Newborn," *The American Rhythm: Studies* by Mary Austin, © 1923 and 1930, renewed © 1950 by Harry Mera, Kenneth M. Chapman and Mary C. Wheelwright, revised edition © renewed by Kenneth M. Chapman and Mary C. Wheelwright. "Elegy for the Giant Tortoises" from *Selected Poems,* by Margaret Atwood. Copyright © 1976. Reprinted by permission of Houghton Mifflin Company.

Excerpts from *Song of the Dream People* by James Houston © 1972. Reprinted by permission of James Houston.

Rochelle Wallace, "Raven Sweat," from *In Context: A Quarterly of Sustainable Culture,* No. 24, 1990.

Inspiration House Publications for Winston Abbott's *Have You Heard the Cricket Song?*, 1971. Reprinted by permission of the publisher.

Ishpriya R.S.C.J., © 1984, "Flowers," "Sandhya," and "Water" from *Kalkalnadini (The Singing of the Stream)*, Jeevan-Dhara Ashram Society, Jaihari Khal, Garhwal Himalayas, 1984.

Dolores La Chapelle for "We give away our thanks" from *Earth Festivals: Seasonal Celebrations for Everyone Young and Old*, by Dolores La Chapelle, Silverton, CO, Finn Hill Arts, 1974. Reprinted by permission of the author.

W. E. R. La Farge, "i: earth's song," © 1980 from *The Changing & Unchanging Harvest*, Heartwork Press. Reprinted by permission of the author.

Robert Aitken, "Gatha 183," from *The Dragon Who Never Sleeps: Verse for Zen Buddhist Practice*, Larkspur Press. Diamond Sangha © 1990. Reprinted by permission of the author.

Liveright Publishing Corporation for e.e. cummings, *Xiape* © 1926. Reprinted by permission of the publisher.

Robert MacLean © 1985, *Heartwood*, Finn Hill Arts, Silverton, Colorado.

Excerpts from *Collected Poems and Plays* by Rabindranath Tagore (New York: Macmillan & Co., 1937).

Medical Mission Sisters © 1965. "Spirit of God," East African Missionaries.

Ralph Metzner, "Gaia's Alchemy: Ruin and Renewal of the Elements," *Revision*, vol. 9, No. 2, Spring, 1987

N. Scott Momaday for "The Delight Song of Tsoai-Talee" from *Songs from this Earth on Turtle's Back*, edited by Joseph Bruchac, Greenfield Review Press, Greenfield Center, NY, 1983. Copyright © 1983 by N. Scott Momaday.

William Morrow & Co., Inc. for excerpts from *Sacred Path: Spells, Prayers and Power Songs of the American Indians*, edited by John Bierhorst © 1983; for excerpt from *Heaven's Breath: A Natural History of the Wind*, by Lyall Watson, © 1984 by Lyall Watson. Reprinted by permission of William Morrow & Co., Inc.

Excerpts from *The Bible*, New Revised Standard Version. Thomas Nelson Publishers, Nashville, TN, 1989.

445

New American Library, a division of Penguin Books USA for excerpt from Fyodor Dostoyevsky's *The Brothers Karamazov*, translated by Constance Garnett, 1980. Reprinted by permission of the publisher.

New Directions Publishing Corporation for the following: Dylan Thomas, *Poems of Dylan Thomas*, © 1939 by New Directions Corporation. Denise Levertov, *Candles in Babylon*, © 1982 by Denise Levertov. Gary Snyder, *Turtle Island*, © 1968 by Gary Snyder. William Everson, *The Residual Years*, © 1948 by New Directions Publishing Corporation. Denise Levertov, *The Freeing of the Dust*, © 1975 by Denise Levertov. Denise Levertov, *Breathing the Water*, © 1987 by Denise Levertov. Gary Snyder, *Regarding Wave*, © 1970 by Gary Snyder. Thomas Merton, *Raids on the Unspeakable*, © 1966 The Abbey of Gethsemani Inc.

New Society Publishers for Barbara Deming's "Spirit of Love," *A Barbara Deming Reader*, 1984; Ellen Bass, *Our Stunning Harvest*, 1985; John Seed and Joanna Macy in *Thinking Like a Mountain: Toward a Council of All Beings*, 1988. Reprinted by permission of New Society Publishers, (800) 333-9093.

North Point Press for excerpts: From *A Part*: "A Purification," "We Who Prayed and Wept," "Woods," "Another Descent," and "Ripening." From *Collected Poems*: "Manifesto: The Mad Farmer Liberation Front," "Prayers and Sayings of the Mad Farmer #2, #8, #9," and "Song (4)." From *Break the Mirror*: "Just Enough" and "A Love Letter." From *The Language of the Birds*: "The Canticle for Brother Sun." From *The Selected Poems of Shuntaro Tanikawa*: "Spring." From *Left Out in the Rain*: "Gatha for all Beings." Excerpted from *A Part*, © 1980 by Wendell Berry; *Collected Poems* © 1984 by Wendell Berry; *Break the Mirror* © 1987 by Nanao Sakaki; *The Language of the Birds* © 1984 edited by David Guss; *The Selected Poems of Shuntaro Tanikawa* © 1983 by Harold Wright (translator); *Left Out in the Rain* © 1986 by Gary Snyder.

W. W. Norton & Co., Inc. for "Easter Morning" and the lines from "The Invocation to Kali" are reprinted from *Collected Poems (1930–1973)* by May Sarton by permission of W. W. Norton & Co., Inc. © 1974 by May Sarton.
W. W. Norton & Co., for "Autumn Day," *Translations from the Poetry of Rainer Maria Rilke*, by M.D. Herter Norton, 1938. Reprinted by permission of W. W. Norton & Co., Inc.

Ohio University Press for "On the Way" by Ho Chi Minh, from *Reflections from Captivity*, translated by Christopher Jenkins, Tran Khanh Tuyet, and Huynh Sanh Thong, edited by David Marr, 1978. Reprinted by permission of the publisher.

Orbis Books for John S. Mbiti's "A Litany for Rain," *How the Other Third Lives: Third World Stories, Songs, Prayers, and Essays from Asia, Africa, and Latin America*, edited by Margaret B. White and Robert N. Quigley, 1977. Reprinted by permission of the publisher.

Oxford University Press for *The Oxford Book of Prayer*, edited by George Appleton, 1985. Reprinted by permission of Oxford University Press on behalf of the author.

Leopold Sédar Senghor, "Prayer for Peace," Part V, abridged, from *The Selected Poems of Leopold Sédar Senghor*, translated by John Reed and Clive Wake, Oxford University Press, © 1964. Reprinted by permission of Oxford University Press and Georges Borchardt, Inc.

Oxford University Press Canada for "Elegy for the Giant Tortoises" from *Selected Poems*, by Margaret Atwood. Copyright © 1976. Reprinted by permission of Oxford University Press Canada.

Parallax Press for excerpts from *Being Peace* by Thich Nhat Hanh, edited by Arnold Kotler, 1987. Reprinted by permission of publisher and author.
Parallax Press for excerpts from *Present Moment, Wonderful Moment, Mindfulness Verse for Daily Living* by Thich Nhat Hanh, 1990. Reprinted by permission of publisher and author.

"Escape," *The Complete Poems of D. H. Lawrence*. Copyright © 1964, 1971 by Angelo Ravagli and C. M. Weekley, Executors of the Estate of Frieda Lawrence Ravagli. Used by permission of Viking Penguin, a division of Penguin Books, USA.

Perivale Press for Maria Eugenia Vaz Ferreira's "A Furtive Glass," in *Open to the Sun: A Bilingual Anthology of Latin-American Women Poets*, edited by Nora Jacquez Wieser, 1979.

Laurence Pollinger Limited for an excerpt from *The Plumed Serpent*, by D. H. Lawrence. Reprinted by permission of Laurence Pollinger Ltd. and the Estate of Frieda Lawrence Ravagli.

Jeff Poniewaz for "Whalewisdompeace Illumination," in *Dolphin Leaping in the Milky Way*, Inland Ocean Books, 4540 S. First St., Milwaukee, WI 53207. Reprinted by permission of the author.

447

Princeton University Press for Chan-jan, from Fung Ya-lan's *A History of Chinese Philosophy, Vol. 2,* 1953. Reprinted by permission of the publisher.

From *No Foreign Land* by Wilfred Pelletier & Ted Poole. © 1973 by Wilfred Pelletier & Ted Poole. Reprinted by permission of Pantheon Books, a division of Random House, Inc.

Excerpts from *The Rain in the Trees* by W. S. Merwin. © 1988 by W. S. Merwin. Reprinted by permission of Alfred A. Knopf, Inc.

"Late Summer" by Theokritos and "Cicada" by an anonymous Hellenistic poet, from *Sappho and the Greek Lyric Poets,* translated by Willis Barnstone. © 1962, 1967, 1988 by Willis Barnstone. Reprinted by permission of Schocken Books, published by Pantheon Books, a division of Random House, New York, 1988.
From *The Plumed Serpent,* by D. H. Lawrence. Copyright 1926 by Alfred A. Knopf, Inc. Reprinted by permission of Alfred A. Knopf, Inc.

Jacquetta Hawkes for version of Pharaoh Akhenaten's "Hymn to the Sun," from *Man in the Sun,* by Jacquetta Hawkes, Random House, Inc. 1962. Reprinted by permission of author.

"The Negro Speaks of Rivers," copyright © 1926 by Alfred A. Knopf, Inc., and renewed 1954 by Langston Hughes. Reprinted from *Selected Poems of Langston Hughes* by permission of the publisher.

From *To Serve the Devil: Natives & Slaves,* edited by Paul Jacobs, Saul Landau, and Eve Pell. Copyright © 1971 by Paul Jacobs and Saul Landau. Reprinted by permission of Random House, Inc., and the Joan Daves Agency.

"Return," *Selected Poems* by Robinson Jeffers, Random House, Inc. Copyright © 1965.

Reprinted with permission of Charles Scribner's Sons, an imprint of Macmillan Publishing Company, from *Poems Old & New* by John Hall Wheelock, © 1936 by Charles Scribner's Sons, renewed 1964 by John Hall Wheelock.

The following were reprinted by arrangement with Shambhala Publications, Inc., 300 Massachusetts Ave., Boston, MA 02115. From *First Thought, Best Thought* by Chöyam Trungpa © 1983. From *Nine-Headed Dragon River* by Peter Matthiessen, © 1985. From *The Bodhisattva of Compassion* by John Blofield, © 1988. From *Tassajara*

Recipe Book by Ed Brown, Shambhala, 1985. Lama Govinda, *The Way of the White Clouds*, Shambhala, Berkeley, 1971. Reprinted by permission of Unwin Hyman Ltd.

Rabbi Rami M. Shapiro for excerpts from *Tangents: Selected Poems 1978–1988*, ENR Wordsmiths, Miami, 1988, and *New Traditions*, Miami, © 1986. Reprinted by permission of author.

Simon & Schuster for excerpts from John Lame Deer and Richard Erdoes, *Lame Deer Seeker of Visions*, © 1972 by John Lame Deer and Richard Erdoes. Reprinted by permission of Simon & Schuster, Inc.

Stanford University Press for Hsiao Kango's "Change," translated by Henry H. Hart, in *A Garden of Peonies: Translations of Chinese Poems into English Verse*, 1938. Reprinted by permission of publisher.

Sunstone Press for excerpt from *Songs of the Tewa* by Herbert J. Spinden, 1976. Reprinted by permission of publisher.

Threshold Books for excerpts from Rumi's *Open Secret*, translated by John Moyne & Colman Barks, 1984. Reprinted by permission of the publisher.

Nanao Sakaki, "Why," *Real Play*, Tooth of Time Books, Santa Fe, 1981.

Reprinted by permission of publishers and the Trustees of Amherst College, from *The Poems of Emily Dickinson*, edited by Thomas D. Johnson, Belknap Press of Harvard University Press, © 1951, 1955, 1979, 1983 by the President and Fellows of Harvard College.

University of California Press, for excerpts from *Mantramanjari, The Vedic Experience* by Raimundo Panikkar with the collaboration of N. Shanta, M. Rogers, B. Baumer, M. Bidoli, © 1977 by Raimundo Panikkar; and from Rainer Maria Rilke, *Duino Elegies*, trans./ed. by C. F. MacIntyre, "The Ninth Elegy," © 1961 C. F. MacIntyre. Reprinted with permission by University of California Press.

From *The Tewa World: Space, Time, and Becoming in Pueblo Society* by Alfonso Ortiz (Chicago: University of Chicago Press). © 1964 by University of Chicago Press. All rights reserved. Reprinted by permission of the publisher.

University of Massachusetts Press for material reprinted from *Prayers for Dark People* by W. E. B. Du Bois, edited by Herbert Aptheker (Amherst: University of Massachusetts Press, 1980). © 1980 by The University of Massachusetts Press.

449

"In No Way," "In the Garden," "One Leaf," and "Kaddish," by David Ignatow, © 1982 by David Ignatow. Reprinted from *New & Collected Poems 1970–1985*; "On the Mountain: A Conversation," © 1987 by J. P. Seaton and James Cryer. Reprinted from *Bright Moon, Perching Bird: Poems by Li Po and Tu Fu*, translated from the Chinese by J. P. Seaton and James Cryer. Used by permission of University of New England Press.

"The Heaven of Animals" by James Dickey, © 1961. Reprinted from *James Dickey Poems 1957–1961*, University of New England Press. This poem first appeared in *The New Yorker* magazine.

From *Pre-Colombian Literature of Mexico* by Miguel Leon-Portilla. Translated from the Spanish by Grace Lobanov and Miguel Leon-Portilla. © 1969 by the University of Oklahoma Press. Reprinted by permission of the publisher.

"Dead Man's Song" reprinted from *Eskimo Poems from Canada and Greenland*, translated by Tom Lowenstein, by permission of the University of Pittsburgh Press. © 1973 by Tom Lowenstein. Reprinted by permission of the publisher.

Navajo, "A Prayer of the Night Chant," *Native American Traditions*, edited by Sam Gill, Wadsworth Publishing, California.

Diann Neu, co-director of "WATER": Women's Alliance for Theology, Ethics and Ritual, 8035 13th St., Silver Spring, MD 20910. Reprinted with permission of the author.

"Transmutation," by Antoinette Adam, from *Weavings*, Vol. III, No. 3, May/June 1987. © 1987 Antoinette Adam. Used by permission of the author.

White Pine Press for Han-Shan, "The View from Cold Mountain," *Poems of Han-Shan and Shih-te*, translated by Arthur Tobias, James Sanford, and J. P. Seaton, edited by Dennis Maloney, 1982. Reprinted with permission of publisher.

"The Poet Prays to the Loba," from *Loba, Parts I–VIII*, by Diane di Prima, Wingbow Press, Berkeley, © 1978 by Diane di Prima.

Wolfe Publishing Ltd. for "Let Us Be United," from Rig Veda, *Prayers for the Future of Mankind*, edited by Salomons, © Wolfe Publishing Ltd., 1975.

Paul Winter © 1982 "Canticle of the Sun," on *Missa Gaia*, Living Music Records, Inc.